RHYMERS

CURRICULUM GUIDE

Books may be purchased in quantity and/or special sales by contacting the publisher,

4402 23rd Street Suite #301
Long Island City, NY 11101
(718) 937-BEAT (2328)
info@beatglobal.org

Published by: BEAT Press, Ltd, Queens, New York
Written by: Yogi "Y?" Guyadin
Edited by: John Bass Tournas, Richard Hauser Jr., Yves "Human" Jerome, Anna Diorio, JLove Calderón, Cecilia Cruz, and Matia Burnett.
Creative Direction by: Yves "Human" Jerome
Layout by: Gabriel Freitas
Cover Design by: Hebron Warren

ISBN: 9780997523508

1. Education
First Edition
Printed in US by CreateSpace

ENDORSEMENTS

"BEAT's cypher philosophy keeps to the roots of street culture of New York City, which I have witnessed and captured with my camera over the years"
— **Jamel Shabazz**, Educator, Visual Storyteller, Hip Hop Documentarian

"The BEAT curricula is fire! It allows youth to live their art and express their creativity."
— **Mutulu Olugbala** aka M1 of dead prez, MC, Activist, and Conscious Content Producer

"As a Hip Hop pedagogue and artist focused on equipping students with critical lenses and expressive skills sets while building creative community, I find The Beat Rhymers Curriculum to be an incredibly valuable tool. It inspires action, engagement and personal development organically, honestly and authentically with respect to the Cypher, the Hip Hop Elements and the magic of participants."
— **Rabbi Darkside** (né Samuel Sellers); MC/DJ/Beatboxer/ Educator, Professor of Hip Hop Pedagogy & Practice at The New School, U.S. Dept of State Cultural Arts Ambassador.

"What is innovative about the program are the principles that are taught within the musical skills they learn— fairness, listening, discipline, honouring your truth."
→ **Toni Blackman**, Rapper, Actress, Writer, Founder of Freestyle Union, and first Hip Hop Ambassador to the U.S. State Department

"If not for the Beat Rhymers program coming into our school last year, I can say with confidence that at least three of our students would have dropped out this year."
— **Tom Mullen**, former Assistant Principal, East Side Community High School

"These programs are the first of its kind that pay attention to what the students actually want to learn. The programs are relevant to today's student."
— **Monique Flores**, Director, University Settlement Beacon's High School"

TABLE OF CONTENTS

INTRODUCTION

You are now holding in your hands not only a curriculum, but a guide book and instruction manual to give your students the tools to confidently self express and identify themselves through the power of the word and Hip Hop. This curriculum was not born in a boardroom or a think tank. It is the result of the trials and successes BEAT Global has experienced from pioneering the Beat Rhymers program in New York City and witnessing the positive impact the program has had on our students. It is a result of giving true Hip Hop practitioners a platform to authentically teach, share knowledge, and affect young people in our communities. Ultimately, the curriculum is a result of our will and desire to carry on the tradition of storytelling through music, practicing one of Hip Hop's oldest tenets which ensures the art and skill of MC'ing is passed on from one generation to the next — "Each One, Teach One". We, Hip Hop's global citizens, are responsible for the preservation of Hip Hop culture. Consider this curriculum as a tool-building mechanism to honor and carry on that tradition and instill the universal values of peace, love, unity, and having fun.

What is truly powerful is just how qualified and talented your students already are. Every individual is born an artist full of curiosity and creativity. The Beat Rhymers Curriculum is a means to unleash artistry through a series of interactive exercises, games, lesson plans, and homework. The purpose is to awaken, nurture, and encourage creativity and collaboration regardless of who your students are; regardless of race, social, political, or economic circumstances — these methods of self-expression are universal. This curriculum is also a step towards truly embodying Hip Hop as a mindset, lifestyle, and an identity. Hip Hop is not exclusive to a genre of music, type of fashion, or a particular vernacular. Hip Hop can no longer be boxed into the trappings of traditional definitions, or the "four elements" of rapping, breaking, graffiti writing, and DJ'ing. As Hip Hop pioneer, activist, artist, and living legend KRS-1 expressed, Hip Hop existed long before the definitions we have created, and Hip Hop will continue to evolve and grow. Hip Hop is truly a progressive school of thought and an unstoppable creative self-expression in the face of challenges and oppression. It is a mindset that is enabling, creative, and inspires resourcefulness in students which they can apply to all areas of their lives.

Whether it be writing, rapping, dancing, or beatboxing, the only tools needed are imagination and dedication to the craft. Think of this curriculum as a map and you, the instructor, are the compass who guides your students to discover and navigate their inherent creativity. Let the journey begin!

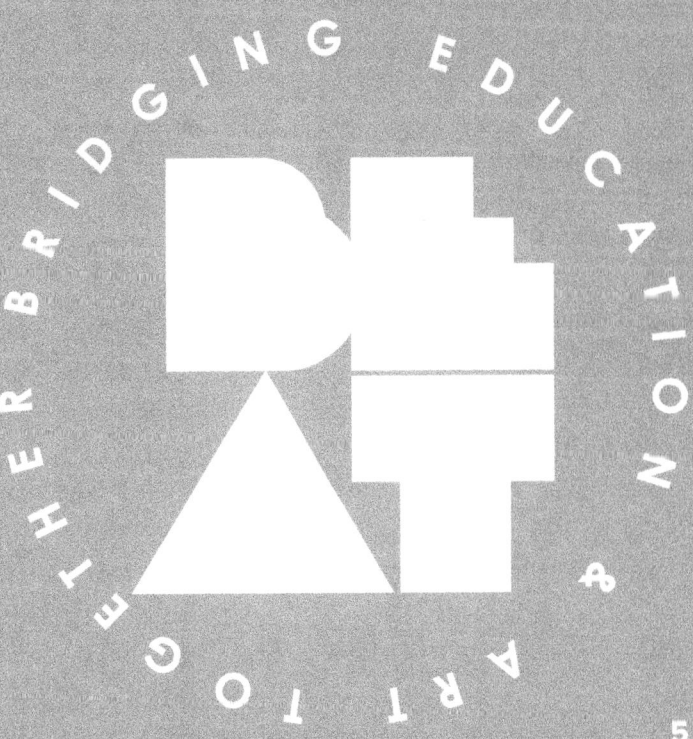

BRIDGING EDUCATION ART TOGETHER

ADDRESSING THE COMMON CORE STATE STANDARDS

As you may already know, the Common Core State Standards (CCSS) for English Language Arts and Mathematics were implemented in 2010 to ensure consistent educational standards across grade levels, disciplines, and states. Additionally, the Common Core Standards ensure that students are prepared for the challenges of college and careers. Whether students decide to matriculate into college right after graduation, take a break, attend trade school, or go straight to work, the CCSS aims to provide 21st century life and career skills necessary for success. Rather than teach students rote memorization, the goal of the Common Core State Standards is to emphasize critical thinking, creativity, and the ability to apply classroom-learned skills and knowledge to real-world problems. These elements are critical to a Beat Rhymers class. By incorporating Common Core Standards into this curriculum, our commitment is to equip educators with the best possible practices to amplify their impact on students in these vital areas.

Despite the controversy around the Common Core State Standards, BEAT has chosen to include CCSS in order to make it widely accessible for educators and relevant to modern concerns. We recognize, respect and acknowledge the valuable efforts of advocacy groups against the Common Core, who are similarly striving to create a level playing field for all students. Whether or not you support the Common Core, you will find that the BEAT Curriculum is for you. If you want to implement a set of standards-aligned activities, we have ensured that each lesson is anchored in relevant standards. If, however, you decide that the Common Core is not for you, you can still use the Curriculum without sacrificing its original intent – to cultivate students' passion for music while fostering the development of valuable life skills.

There are five key components of the Common Core State Standards for English Language Arts: Reading, Writing, Speaking & Listening, Language, and Media & Technology*. These are known as the Anchor Standards, and they represent the benchmark skills that students are expected to master at each grade level. Each of the Anchor Standards emphasize literacy and teach students to solve problems and make connections using an interdisciplinary lens.

Students who have mastered the Anchor Standards exhibit the following:

- **Demonstrate independence** – *Students can work through complex texts, narratives, and speakers' points-of-view with very little support.*

- **Build strong content knowledge** – *Students can build a strong base of knowledge across disciplines and different content areas.*

- **Respond to the varying demands of audience, task, purpose, and discipline** – *Students can adapt their communication to fit a variety of audiences, tasks, and purposes.*

- **Comprehend as well as critique** – *Students become efficient readers and listeners, and can think critically about the information they are presented.*

- **Value evidence** – *Students can support their claims and ideas with substantive evidence.*

- **Use technology and digital media strategically and capably** – *Students can use media and technology to enhance their reading, writing, language, speaking, and listening skills, and can present information in novel ways.*

- **Understand other perspectives and cultures** – *Students appreciate diversity, varying points-of-view, and can collaborate with others despite their differences.*

In addition to English Language Arts standards, The Beat Rhymers Curriculum offers a wealth of unexpected benefits in learning math via music theory. The Common Core State Standards also focus on a clear set of mathematical concepts and skills that students are expected learn and understand as they progress through the grades. These concepts and skills hone students' higher-order thinking skills and encourage them to solve real-world problems. Rather than focus on grade-specific math subjects, we've aligned each of the lessons with the Standards for Mathematical Practice (SMP). For a comprehensive list and description of each of the Anchor Standards and Standards for Mathematical Practice, refer to Appendix A in this manual.

HOW TO READ COMMON CORE STATE STANDARDS

As you will notice in the Appendix, the Common Core State Anchor Standards are written as follows:

CCSS.ELA-LITERACY.CCRA. R

CCSS.ELA-LITERACY.CCRA. W

CCSS.ELA-LITERACY.CCRA. SL

CCSS.ELA-LITERACY.CCRA. L

These represent four of the five key components (or strands) of the Common Core State Standards for English Language Arts: Reading, Writing, Speaking and Listening, and Language. The fifth component, Media and Technology, is integrated into the other standards, as it is inextricably linked to every aspect of a 21ˢᵗ century student's learning experience. Media and Technology standards include students' ability to use digital tools and media to enhance learning, develop new products, and to present information.

So, what do the letters in the CCSS represent? Take this example:

CCSS.ELA-LITERACY.CCRA. R

1. CCSS
Represents the Framework (Common Core).

2. ELA-LITERACY
Represents the section of the Common Core from which the standard comes.

3. CCRA
Represents the status, in this case, A is for Anchor.

4. R
Represents the strand, in this case, R eading.

5. 1
Represents the Anchor Standard, which tells you exactly what skill students should master.

As you move through The Beat Rhymers Curriculum, you will notice that each lesson is aligned to a set of specific Common Core Anchor Standards and Standards for Mathematical Practice, indicated by a mix of letters and numbers. You may refer to Appendix B in this manual for a complete description of each of the alignments in each lesson. While each lesson may be aligned with more standards than we've indicated, please note that we've focused on core skills in each lesson.

Are you interested in additional standards or specific skillsets for your students' level and ability? A comprehensive list is available at the CCSS website at h ttp://www.corestandards.org. In Appendix C, we offer a set of Common Core alignments in Literacy and Math which can be used to develop musical activities and lessons for your students across grade levels.

We are confident that as you use The Beat Rhymers Curriculum, you'll be inspired to discover new ways to engage your students and infuse your activities with key skills like collaboration, communication, creativity, and critical thinking.

Enjoy the process!

NOTE TO EDUCATORS

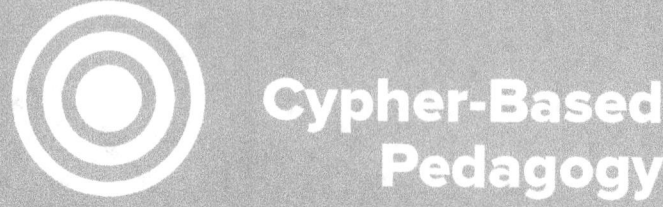

Cypher-Based Pedagogy

You find yourself walking into a Beat Rhymers classroom. The entire class is standing in a circle clapping rhythmically while students and instructors take turns rapping, singing, beatboxing, or playing an instrument. In between turns, they all chant "two bars and pass, two bars and pass, two bars and pass make the cypher last!" One instructor sees that you've been observing, and motions for you to join the circle. "My friend, there are no observers in a BEAT class — only participants."

Grounded in Hip Hop[1] ideology, and applicable to anyone interested in creative expression, the following curriculum developed by BEAT instructors and staff involves a model of Cypher-Based Pedagogy™. For centuries, humans have gathered in circle for ceremony, honoring tradition, and cultivation of community. The cypher is no different, embodying the concepts of equal communication, respect, and the creation of a safe space where all feel comfortable sharing their ideas, art, and personal experiences. In the formative years and to this day, cyphering is crucial to the development of the core elements of Hip Hop culture: MCing, beatboxing, DJing, graffiti, and Bboying. Recognizing the cypher as the breeding ground for these art forms, The Beat Rhymers Curriculum applies the same principles to allow creativity and respect to flourish. We have found that the creation of this environment is essential for inspiring individual and collaborative artistic expression in youth anywhere around the world. Because this is a Cypher-Based curriculum, you are not the "leader" of the group. Instead, you are an equal member of the community playing the role of facilitator. As such, your responsibility is to work with your students to create an environment of openness and equality, while also learning from the group. You will be both a teacher and student, participating actively and giving others the floor.

What if you could radically shift your relationship to your students to be one of reciprocity, love, joy? BEAT Cypher-Based curriculum is carefully crafted to fully bring this transformation into your classroom, your life, and the lives of your students.

We strongly encourage you to participate in activities along with your students. The greatest teacher is also a student. In order for students to truly learn and internalize material, allow the knowledge to flow both ways. This has been proven to stimulate a deeper internalization of content. When giving instructions for an activity, it is important to be concise. This leaves ample room for your students to find their own avenues of connection. Surprise yourself and your students. If a student knows the activity, open the space for the student to explain it to the class. Similarly, it is always better to stimulate learning and discussion by asking questions rather than making statements. Take every opportunity that you come across to give your students power over their own learning. What else can you do to activate learning and discussion in your class? This is the aim of The Beat Rhymers Curriculum.

To ensure that the class runs smoothly, we have a set of basic guidelines for implementation:

● In many Beat Rhymers classes, swearing in a musical context is not expressly prohibited. It is unfair to ask young artists to censor their art. However, it is fair to ask your students to respect each other and you. Swearing aimed to insult another or other forms of disrespect outside of a musical context (for example, directed at another student) should not be tolerated. This creates a safe space for all students to express themselves without fear of judgment.

● One Mic Rule: When someone is talking no one else should be. Respect is always important.

---

[1] KRS-One writes, " As I have stated for several years now; we are not just doing Hip Hop, we are Hip Hop! Therefore, we cannot spell our lifestyle in lower case letters. We are referred to as Hip Hoppas and we have the right as well as the responsibility to define ourselves. I suggest we spell the name of our culture, our community, our nation, and even ourselves as either HipHop or as Hip Hop, but never as hip-hop." KRS makes a good point; this culture is tied to our identities, and so we choose to spell it capitalized like this to empower each other and our shared culture.

As an educator, proficiency in any type of musical or writing medium is highly recommended. Are you interested in sharing this material with your students but have no musical training? Have no fear! You will be able to use these lessons to develop your skills and create content alongside your students! Bringing in a guest artist to support the curriculum can also be a powerful way to excite and engage your students while providing clarity and setting an example of excellence. In the spirit of the cypher, there will be several points throughout the curriculum where you will be asked to perform and demonstrate your skills for the students.

In the first paragraph of this section, the scene includes students not only rapping, but also singing, beatboxing, and playing instruments. While this curriculum welcomes all artistically driven students, most of its activities focus on songwriting and vocal performance for the verbal communication of ideas. No one should be discouraged from participating, but it should be made clear from the start that students who are interested in instrumental music will have to contribute vocally as well. The goal of this curriculum is to provide the musical tools for students so that after the class, they feel empowered to continue making their own music without the guidance and structure of a class.

How to use this book

The Beat Rhymers Curriculum consists of 25 lessons broken down into 5 units. Each unit builds off the concepts and skills taught in the one before. Unit 1 is called **Building From The Ground Up** , and is mainly focused on introducing students to the class, the teacher, and one another. Unit 2 is called **Fundamentals : Tools Of The Trade** where students will be introduced to the basic musical tools and techniques that they will use throughout the curriculum. Unit 3 is called **Collaboration: Let's Flip This** , and focuses on allowing students to utilize the concepts from the previous unit in the security of a group setting. From here, students will be allowed to work on their own individual projects in Unit 4, which is called **Individual Songwriting: Know Thy Self** , and finally hone their performance skills in Unit 5, which is called **Performance: Rock The Mic**. The cumulative nature of these units is essential. Do not move on to a new unit, lesson, or activity if you feel the knowledge and skills were not understood. It is much better for one activity to last an entire class period than for you to rush through and leave students confused.

In each **Lesson** , there is a list of **Objectives** , which are the goals of the **Activities** contained in each Lesson plan. Each Lesson is designed to span 45-60 minutes, and at the beginning of each plan, you will see a list of **Materials** that you will need to have ready for that class period. Each activity has its own estimated time length, setting (where students should be standing/sitting, and what materials they should have ready), and a brief description of what the activity involves. Some activities will have a **Tone** suggestion. In general, the tone of every Beat Rhymers activity should encourage fun and inclusivity. All members of the class should be encouraged to contribute their skills and talents to the class. Following this, the actual structure and process of the activity are laid out in bullet points.

At the end of each lesson, there may be a small section labeled **Homework** and/or **Extension Activity**. These can be used as material for students to work on outside of class, or as extra work if your class finishes the lesson plan activities early. Additionally, homework can be used to challenge an advanced class beyond the requirements of the normal lesson plan. We believe that homework should be minimal and only assigned when it is an important addition to the lesson. In many of our classes, we have found that students can be overburdened by work for other classes, extra curricular activities, social life, family obligations, and job commitments, to name a few. Unnecessary homework only serves to distract students from learning the essential material. It reduces a class in which students are free to express themselves and grow in their creativity to another academic commitment they must complete before they move on to the next step in life. For this reason, Beat Rhymers homework is minimal and should not be forced upon your young people. We do, however, encourage students to work on performance material outside of class. You will find that students who are properly motivated and engaged in the class will take it upon themselves to do the extra legwork to master the material outside of class.

The last lesson in Units 1-4 ends with **Performance Time**. This is the period of time where students will perform using the material they learned and worked on in the unit. Each Performance Time is followed by a discussion, where the teacher and class can offer constructive criticism to each student. We have made a conscious decision to mention a suggested time frame for each Performance Time, yet we believe it should be up to the teacher to determine how long the performance will be. Perhaps the show went really well, and the students are eager to perform again after discussing what they could improve on. In this case, a second or longer performance is fine. However, in classes with Performance Time, we recommend devoting at least half the class period to performance, leaving room for a second or longer performance. Performance Time does not need to take place in an auditorium with a stage; the classroom or any large, open space is fine. Unit 5 does not end with a Performance Time. Lessons 24 and 25 are rehearsals for the final show, which should take place in an auditorium or somewhere where the students can have an audience other than members of the Beat Rhymers class.

We recommend that you read each lesson plan at least a day or two before the class when you plan to use it, as there are often preparations you want to make before each class begins.

Each of these lessons has been carefully curated to span the prescribed 45-60 minutes of class time. However, because every teacher and body of students are different, you may find yourself with some extra time to spend. Don't stress! We believe that these opportunities are perfect times to relax, for your students to talk in an unstructured way about their lives and their art, especially in the context of the collaboration unit, having the class comfortable with one another is essential. After each unit, feel free to use the provided Notes section to reflect on the progress of your class, make preparations for the following unit, or just collect your thoughts.

Before you begin

It is important that you possess a working knowledge of Hip Hop culture, and specifically MCing, before you begin this course. This does not mean that you must speak in slang, dress in a certain way, or project yourself in any way outside of who you really are. In fact, it's simply not Hip Hop to claim an identity that is not your own. Rather, you must overstand, respect, and believe in the art and culture to be able to teach this curriculum, and to represent the values embedded within. If you are an instructor without experience in Hip Hop you will be able to use any knowledge of spoken word, poetry, creative writing, singing/songwriting, music theory, composition and theater to assist you with this curriculum. We high-

ly encourage you to use any of your artistic skills, whether it be sharing a poem you wrote or singing a song you created to connect to this curriculum and your students. Even if you do not consider yourself an artist, you can participate in the activities and sharing portions of the lesson plans.

This section will provide our own brief history of Hip Hop music and several resources to help you familiarize yourself with the culture, its origins, where it is today, and the people that live it. While we could have included suggested songs, times change rapidly, so the music that you use is entirely contingent on what your students are interested in. Ask them who they listen to, and create a playlist, do research on the music and lyrics, and make sure not to let your opinions lead the class. In fact, it's an opportunity to meet the students where they genuinely are.

A Brief History

Before there were rappers and producers, beats and rhymes, there were DJs. In the 1970s in the South Bronx neighborhood of New York City, these musicians would throw huge parties at parks and community centers. Using two turntables, vinyl disks, and powerful amplification systems, these DJs would spin anything from soul, to funk, to disco, to get the crowds dancing. One of these musicians, DJ Kool Herc, made a revolutionary discovery at one of these parties: there were certain parts of songs (most often when the recording would feature solely a drum beat) that made the crowd go wild, dance harder, and cheer louder. In using two copies of the same record, one on each turntable, he found he could loop these drum breaks indefinitely to give the crowd exactly what they wanted. This marked the beginning of the beat.

As DJs continued perfecting the practice of looping beats, they began to enlist the help of MCs to keep the crowd's interest and energy up. These MCs would use call-and-response, rhyming, and other performance tactics to spice up the DJ's show. As this practice began to proliferate, and MCs began recording their rhymes, what was previously viewed as a support act for the DJ grew into an art form of its own. Meanwhile, other art forms began to assimilate themselves into the same culture: graffiti artists would spray paint to make the rubble and desolation of their neighborhoods beautiful, breakers developed new and dynamic styles of movement in response to Kool Herc's concept of the "break," and vocal percussionists called beatboxers provided percussion with their bodies so that rappers could freestyle on the corner without the need for a sound system.

Fast forward 40 years. Today, Hip Hop music is so expansive that it defies simple categorization; DJing and beatmaking have become two distinct art forms, rappers perform and record with live bands, beatboxers and breakers perform in international competitions, and graffiti art appears in modern art museums. Even from the time this book is published to when you're reading it, significant changes in the landscape and sound of Hip Hop are sure to have occurred. However, while Hip Hop may sound vastly different than it did mere decades ago, there are some cornerstone principles deeply rooted in Hip Hop culture that have remained unchanged. The importance of originality in one's music, the emphasis on mutual respect within the Hip Hop community, and the rhythmic and percussive roots of Hip Hop are all traditional themes that continue to dominate the music and culture.

For a more in depth look into the history of Hip Hop culture and its many forms, check out the suggested resources at the rear of this book.

ACKNOWLEDGEMENTS

We would like to thank all of the wonderful people who have collaborated in order to make this project possible. Firstly, a huge thanks to Beat Rhymers Instructor Y? for his knowledge, patience, and drive to spread the love, as well as to our interns Rich and John who transcribed Y?'s ideas and wrote them up into this volume. Thanks to James Kim for planting this idea to broaden BEAT Global's impact by making BEAT curricula accessible to everyone. Thank you for all that you do to create platforms for talented artists to empower youth across NYC and the world! Thanks to BEAT Global's Creative Director Human for overseeing the creative process, ensuring visuals that reflect the evolution of BEAT Global and guiding the creative department effectively from start to finish. We appreciate you for keeping everyone on track and performing to the best of their abilities.

A very special thanks to our Social Impact Strategist JLove Calderón for her wise advice and guidance through this process and beyond. You are amazing!

Shout out to all of the BEAT Instructors who have taught classes and contributed to this organization, and to all the educators who have seen the worth in our educational ideology.

Finally, massive thanks to all past, present, and future BEAT students! Your creativity, wisdom, and art is an inspiration not only to us but for the rest of the world. Keep spreading the love!

UNIT 1
BUILDING FROM THE GROUND UP

This unit is all about creating a space where students feel comfortable expressing themselves around one another. Especially for an arts-based curriculum in which students will be writing about issues that may be quite personal, it is extremely important that by the end of these five lessons, students feel able to express themselves in front of their peers and work collaboratively towards a common goal. As was mentioned in the Note to Educators, the five units laid out in this curriculum are cumulative, and so must be followed in order, and to completion. The 25 lessons contained in this volume will all work best if your classroom possesses the basic cohesiveness, comfort, and groundwork of respect that Unit 1 is designed to build.

Insofar as your goal to create a space in which students feel comfortable expressing themselves, you would be best served to express yourself with the class. The cypher-based curriculum is most effective when it succeeds in creating a culture of contribution; each member of the cypher contributes equally to the musical performance. Thus the teacher's participation in activities is paramount. We recommend that you begin the semester by introducing yourself to the students through some kind of performance or exhibition of your personal work as it relates to the class.

If you are a musician or dancer, perform for the students. If you are a poet or writer, read them some of your material. If you are an illustrator or photographer, show them one of your works. We have found that if you show the students who you are and what you do, you will be able to better foster an environment in which they feel comfortable expressing themselves in the same way. Share with them personal information about how Hip Hop (or music or art) has impacted your life, and what prompted you to pursue teaching a class on Hip Hop and sharing your knowledge with others.

The best connection you can establish with your students is one that emphasizes your desire to grow along with them, and how that growth is actualized in a class where every member feels comfortable contributing.

Intro to the Beat Rhymers

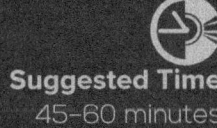

Suggested Time
45–60 minutes

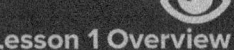

Lesson 1 Overview
Lesson 1 consists of a warm-up activity followed by a discussion on the purpose of the Beat Rhymers class and a free write activity for the students to explore what they want from the class and what they will contribute to the class.

Activities

Activity 1
"Two Bars and Pass, Make the Cypher Last"

Warm Up Activity

- Students get to know each other and the staff

- Students start to feel comfortable expressing themselves openly in front of the class

- Students learn the basics of counting bars in 4/4 time

Activity 2
Beat Rhymers Breakdown

Discussion

Students will have a clear understanding of the purpose of the Beat Rhymers class and know what they will and won't learn as a student

Activity 3
In Giving You Receive

Free Write Exercise

- Students will explore their own aspirations and goals as they relate to the class

- Staff will become familiar with student's skills and interests.

Materials

- **Students**
  - Paper and writing utensils (have these prepared in case your students do not have them)
- **Instructor**
  - Large writing surface with writing utensils

Activity 1

"Two Bars and Pass, Make the Cypher Last"

An introduction exercise for participants to get to know each other.

Time
30–45 minutes

Setting
Everyone stands in a circle facing inwards so that you are visible to one another.

Tone
This should be an upbeat, fun activity. Keep it lively by encouraging the students to be themselves and be friendly with one another.

Description
While getting to know their peers through song and dance, students will be introduced to the methodology of counting bars and how it applies to musical composition and songwriting.

Exercise

● **Round 1**

● Start a clap at a comfortable tempo and repeat the phrase " Two bars and pass, two bars and pass, two bars and pass, make the cypher last. Each bar has two claps: 1, **2**, 3, **4** / 1, **2**, 3, **4** (bold numbers are where the claps land).

▶ Ask each person in the circle to give a name they want to be called and something they love while everyone claps at a consistent tempo. Example (again, bold words denote where the claps land):

" *My name is John, I love cheese pizza!*"

Note It can be very helpful to allow your students to choose a nickname for the class, especially one related to their artistry in some way.

▶ After each person in the circle gives their two bars, the group chants the chorus together: "Two bars and pass, two bars and pass, two bars and pass make the cypher last!"

▶ Explain to the students that this is two bars. The bar is the basic rhythmic metric for most western music, and so it's important that they begin thinking of their lyrics and compositions in this format.

● **Round 2**

▶ Ask the students to repeat the exercise a second time, except this time reciting four bars. Example:

" *My name is Jane, I love science, I play soccer, I go to school!!*"

Note: These rhythmic examples are fairly simple. Students should feel free to speak in any rhythm that they choose over the two or four bar form.

● Remember, each bar has 2 claps: 1, **2** , 3, **4**/ 1, **2** , 3, **4**/ 1, **2** , 3, **4**/ 1, **2** , 3, **4**

Activity 2

Beat Rhymers Breakdown

A brief discussion on the nature of the class.

Time
15–20 minutes

Setting
Students should be seated facing the teacher.

Description
After the students have participated in their first socialization activity, you should give them a good idea of what Beat Rhymers is about — what they will learn in the class, and what they will not learn in the class. We believe it is important to have this discussion on the first day of class to make sure the students know what will be expected of them and if they want what Beat Rhymers has to offer. In short, having this discussion as early as possible maximizes the time spent learning and minimizes the time spent articulating the purpose of the class.

Exercise

● The Beat Rhymers class is broken up into 5 Units, each consisting of 5 lessons. Unit 1, lessons 1-5, is called **Introduction: From The Ground Up**. Here you will get to know your fellow classmates and learn to work together with them, while being introduced to the basics of musical expression. Unit 2, lessons 6-10, is called **Fundamentals: Tools Of The Trade**. Here you will learn the fundamentals of music: basic musicality, writing, improvisation, and performance. Unit 3, lessons 11-15, is called **Collaboration: Let's Flip This**. Here you will learn how to collaborate with your fellow students, and use this skill to create your first piece. Unit 4, lessons 16-20, is called **Individual: Knowledge of Self**. Here you will begin working on a piece that will be developed throughout the next unit. Unit 5, lessons 21-25, is called **Performance: Grab The Mic**. Here you will learn how to perform. You will finish the piece you began working on in the fourth unit and develop a performance around this piece. This class will culminate in a show, planned and developed by you, in which those of you who are willing will have the chance to perform your piece.

- "I want to be clear about what you will and won't learn in the Beat Rhymers class.The purpose of Beat Rhymers is to provide students with a creative platform where they can compose and create original music. Beat Rhymers is not a class for private instrumental instruction. **We will not teach you how to play an instrument**."

- "Though this class places an emphasis on poetry and lyricism, the fundamentals we teach can be used to create any kind of music. They are used by any kind of artist, and are unique only to the act of artistic expression."

- "This class is designed so that individuals with **any level of musical talent can benefit from the class**. Those of you who are instrumentalists, producers, or already talented lyricists will have a chance to share and build upon your skills during the collaborative, individual, and performance portions of the class."

- "The ultimate goal is for you to learn tools and knowledge in this class that will allow you to make music, write songs, contribute to other creative endeavours, find new tools to express yourself fully in all areas of your life, and heighten your creativity outside of the classroom. The most important lesson you can learn in this class is that **you have the right to be an artist**, and that **you have the right to express yourself artistically in any way you so choose**."

● Activity 3

In Giving You Receive

Setting intentions through a free write exercise.

Time
15–30 minutes

Setting
Students should be seated with a surface to write on, every student should have a piece of paper and a pencil/pen.

Description
Free writing is an exercise in self-confidence; by encouraging students to eliminate their inner critic, we foster a welcoming environment where students are more inclined to release self-judgment and share what they feel without holding back. This exercise also encourages students to set specific goals for themselves. By setting goals for the future, we are better able to identify how much and what kind of work needs to be done on a daily basis.

Exercise

"In this class I will give _____ and I will receive _____."

- ● Examples
  - ▶ In this class I will give my attention and I will receive musical knowledge.
  - ▶ In this class I will give respect, and I will receive respect.
  - ▶ In this class I will give my beat rhyming experience to others and I will receive other skills in return.
- ● Give the writing prompt stated above to all of the students.
- ● Give each student a piece of paper for their free write.
- ● Students must free write continuously for 5-10 minutes without stopping. This means no erasing or correcting previous thoughts that have been written. The purpose is to get ideas flowing, unadulterated by an emphasis on spelling.
- ● When they finish, ask them to share their responses with the class. This is important, because reflection often doesn't make an impact until it's vocalized.

Extension Activity

Time
20 minutes

At the end of the "Two Bars and Pass" activity, ask students to repeat something that one of their peers said during the activity. What was the student's name? What did they love? Write those things on the board and ask the students why it is important to create a culture of contribution.

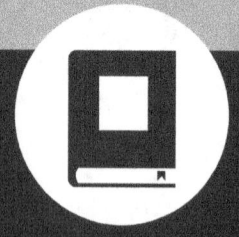

Homework

Students will revise their free write to one page and bring it to the next class. The revised free write will be used in the next class as the basis for a list of rules established by the students for class norms.[2]

---

[2] Unit 1, Lesson 1 Common Core Alignment:
CCSS.ELA-LITERACY.CCRA.W.3–Write narratives to develop real or imagined experiences or events using effective technique, well-chosen details and well-structured event sequences.
CCSS.ELA-LITERACY.CCRA.W.4–Produce clear and coherent writing in which the development, organization, and style are appropriate to task, purpose, and audience.
CCSS.ELA-LITERACY.CCRA.W.10–Write routinely over extended time frames (time for research, reflection, and revision) and shorter time frames (a single sitting or a day or two) for a range of tasks, purposes, and audiences.
CCSS.ELA-LITERACY.CCRA.SL.1–Prepare for and participate effectively in a range of conversations and collaborations with diverse partners, building on others' ideas and expressing their own clearly and persuasively.
CCSS.ELA-LITERACY.CCRA.SL.6–Adapt speech to a variety of contexts and communicative tasks, demonstrating command of formal English when indicated or appropriate.
SMP 7 – Look for and make use of structure

16

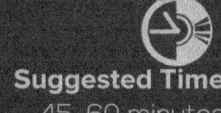

Suggested Time
45–60 minutes

Lesson 2 Overview

Lesson 2 consists of a call-and-response activity to build upon the concept of counting bars in 4/4 time, a follow-up on the free write activity started in Lesson 1, and a "record deal" activity to formulate a contract for the class code of conduct.

Activities

Activity 1
Shabooya!

Call-and-response activity

- Students will build upon the bar and measure system presented in Lesson 1
- Students become more comfortable expressing themselves in front of the class

Activity 2
Free Write Revisited

Discussion

Students will build upon their aspirations and goals for the class

- Staff will become more familiar with students' skills and interests

Activity 3
Need A Deal!

Collaboration on a class code of conduct

Students will establish the classroom as a safe space where they feel comfortable expressing themselves

Materials

- **Students**
  - ▶ Paper and writing utensils
- **Instructor**
  - ▶ Large writing surface with writing utensils

Activity 1

Shabooya!

A call-and-response activity to build upon the concept of counting bars.

Time

15–20 minutes

Setting

Everyone standing in a circle facing inwards.

Tone

This should be an upbeat, fun activity. Keep it lively by encouraging the students to be themselves and be friendly with one another.

Description

Shabooya is a game that involves the musical and oral technique called call-and-response, a form that is often used in Hip Hop and other musical cultures of the African diaspora like Jazz and Blues. It's also an easy and effective element to use in the songwriting process, and so could be useful to your students later on in the course as they begin to write their own pieces. Students will sing a chorus together with the class and then each individual will recite a verse, after which the class again recites the chorus.

Exercise

Welcome everyone back to the class and start by asking if anyone remembers what bars are. We believe in full engagement with our students, so we always encourage our students to show what they learned before showing them. If a student does remember what bars are, have them clap 4 bars at a consistent tempo for the class. If no one remembers what bars are, demonstrate by clapping 4 bars at a consistent tempo yourself. Do not move on until you are sure every student understands what a bar is and can clap any number of them.

- Remember, each bar has two claps. 1, **2**, 3, **4**/ 1, **2**, 3, **4**. Start Shabooya off by clapping on the 2 and 4 of each measure.

- The basic chant goes "Shabooya Sha–Sha Shabooya–Roll Call!"

- The chant will last 2 bars and sounds like "Shabooya **(clap)** Sha–Sha **(clap)** Shabooya– **Roll** Call! **(clap)**" This is chanted by the whole class.

- Immediately after the main chant, an individual

student will say their name and three things that they love, while the class echoes their statements with "What?!

- **Example**
  - ▶ (Call) Johnny: "My name is Johnny" clap
  - ▶ (Response) Class: "What?!" clap
  - ▶ Johnny: "I love to run" clap
  - ▶ Class: "What?!" clap
  - ▶ Johnny: "I love my fam" clap
  - ▶ Class: "What?!" clap
  - ▶ Johnny: "And I love waffles. Roll call!
  - ▶ Class: Shabooya (clap) Sha–Sha (clap) Shabooya–Roll Call!"
  - ▶ (Next student goes, and so on)

Activity 2

Free Write Revisited

A group discussion on the free write assignment given during Lesson 1.

Time
15–20 minutes

Setting
Students should be seated facing the large writing surface while you take notes on it.

Description
The students will revisit their free write assignment from Lesson 1 and share key points with the class. The teacher will record the class contributions on the large writing surface for the class to see. This information will be used in Activity 3 as the basis for a contract outlining the rules and code of conduct that the class must follow.

Exercise

- Ask the students to take out their free writes from last class. Give them 5 to 7 minutes of time to re-examine their free writes and brainstorm anything they would like to add.

- Now ask them to share whatever they would like from their free writes while you record their contributions on the large writing surface.

Activity 3

I Need A Deal!

The students will formulate a contract for appropriate rules of class norms.

Time

15–20 minutes

Setting

Students should be seated facing the large writing surface while you take notes on it.

Description

Use the information you recorded in Activity 2 to prompt students to collaborate on the development of a "record deal" outlining the rules for the classroom.

Exercise

Use the below Discussion Questions to introduce students to the concept of a record deal:

● What is a record deal?

  ▶ For the artist, it's a set of terms and conditions that they and the record company agree on.

  ▶ What would you want to have in your record deal? Why?

"We are going to establish our own record deal between everyone in this class. It will be a code of conduct that we all agree to follow. We want this class to be a safe space where everyone feels comfortable expressing themselves in front of one another."

Further Discussion Questions

What are some things you expressed in your free writes that you think should be included in our record deal?

● What are some things we can put in our record deal to make this class a safe space where everyone feels comfortable expressing themselves?

● Suggested Rules

  ▶ One Mic: Only one person talking at a time.

  ▶ Lateness/Absence rules.

  ▶ Record the students suggested rules for class conduct. Present this list in the form of a record deal contract to the students at the beginning of the next class. They must sign this contract and give it back to the teacher.

HOMEWORK

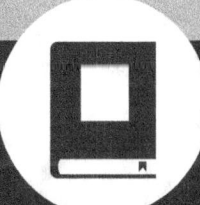

Ask the students to recommend songs whose message resonates with them. The top song can be chosen based on a class vote. Ask the students to listen to it at home and get an idea of what the song is about. Print out the lyrics for students to use in the next class, where the song will be used as an introduction to thematic songwriting.[3]

[3] Unit 1, Lesson 2 Common Core Alignment:
CCSS.ELA-LITERACY.CCRA.SL.1–Prepare for and participate effectively in a range of conversations and collaborations with diverse partners, building on others' ideas and expressing their own clearly and persuasively.
CCSS.ELA-LITERACY.CCRA.SL.2–Integrate and evaluate information presented in diverse media and formats, including visually, quantitatively, and orally.
CCSS.ELA-LITERACY.CCRA.SL.4–Present information, findings, and supporting evidence such that listeners can follow the line of reasoning and the organization, development, and style are appropriate to task, purpose, and audience.
CCSS.ELA-LITERACY.CCRA.W.4–Produce clear and coherent writing in which the development, organization, and style are appropriate to task, purpose, and audience.
CCSS.ELA-LITERACY.CCRA.W.5–Develop and strengthen writing as needed by planning, revising, editing, rewriting, or trying a new approach.
CCSS.ELA-LITERACY.CCRA.R.1–Read closely to determine what the text says explicitly and to make logical inferences from it; cite specific textual evidence when writing or speaking to support conclusions drawn from the text.
SMP 6–Attend to precision
SMP 7–Look for and make use of structure
SMP 8–Look for and express regularity in repeated reasoning

Lesson 3
Off The Top

Suggested Time
45–60 minutes

Lesson 3 Overview
Lesson 3 consists of a call-and-response activity to introduce students to the concept of improvisation, a brief improvisational performance by each student, and an introduction to thematic songwriting.

Activities

Activity 1
The-Reflect-Effect
Call-and-response activity

Introduction to the concept of improvisational performance

Activity 2
Spotlight
30 second improvisational performances

Students will become comfortable improvising in front of their peers

Activity 3
Thinking About Themes

Song lyric analysis

Introduction to thematic songwriting

- Identifying the sections of a song

Materials

- Instructors

  ▸ Today, bring in notebooks or folders for every student in the class. They will be specific to this course, so students should bring them every day.

  ▸ Large writing surface with writing utensils

  ▸ Print out copies of the lyrics chosen in the last class session, enough so that each student gets one.

  ▸ Either a timer, clock, watch, stop watch, or cell phone to track timing.

  ▸ Music player (computer, iPhone, anything that can store and play music) and speakers.

  ▸ Note: If you have a phone or computer you will need to connect the device to speakers via a 1/8" cable.

  ▸ Instrumentals: you will need an internet connection to download the instrumentals in advance or to play from the internet during class. Always ask the students for suggestions on what to play.

  ▸ Print out copies of the "Songwriting Terms" handout provided at the end of this lesson plan.

  ▸ A print out of lyrics from song chosen in previous lesson

  ▸ At the beginning of class, have students sign the contract they developed in the previous lesson. This establishes a concrete agreement between members of the class to follow a code of conduct and get everyone moving together in harmony.

Activity 1

The-Reflect-Effect

A call-and-response activity designed to introduce students to improvisation.

Time
10–15 minutes

Setting
Everyone standing in a circle facing inwards so that you are visible to one another.

Tone
This should be an upbeat, fun activity. Keep it lively by encouraging the students to be themselves and be friendly with one another.

Description
Each student will incorporate motion and sound into an improvisational routine, which the rest of the class will reflect back to them.

Exercise
- Each student should recite their name, then act out a motion while making a sound.

- The group will then mimic their motion and sound together in response.

- **Example**
  - "Johnny!" *bows while making a 'WHOOOSH' sound*
  - The class then repeats this together.
  - After everyone has gone, initiate a discussion:
  - What is improvisation?
  - Definition: to compose, utter, execute, or arrange anything spontaneously, without preparation.
  - Ask students when we have already done improv in previous activities. (i.e. Two Bars and Pass activity)
  - Who are some musicians that are known for their improvisation/freestyling skills?
  - How do you think their ability to freestyle contributes to their creative process?

Activity 2

Spotlight

A 30 second improvisational performance by each student.

Time
15–20 minutes

Setting
Everyone standing in a circle facing inwards so that you are visible to one another.

Tone
This should be an upbeat, fun activity. Keep it lively by encouraging the students to be themselves and be friendly with one another.

Description
Each student will give a 30 second improvisational performance, during which they will talk about whatever they want, without stopping for 30 seconds. Have one of the students who is not performing keep track of time to stop the performer at 30 seconds. This can be a great leadership task for students who are shy or who have excess energy.

Exercise

"In this class I will…"

- Each student will respond to this question with a 30 second improvisational performance.

- The students can incorporate spoken word, singing, rapping, sound-making or beatboxing, and movement into their performance.

- After all the students have performed, initiate a discussion:
  - Which performances stood out to you, or surprised you? Why?
  - What did you notice about individuals' performances, or the class's performance as a whole?
  - How can an individual's performance provide insight into who they are as a person?
  - This section should conclude with discussion on improvisation in general. Encourage the students to recognize the artistic validity of every individual's improvisation; perhaps one student decided to remain silent for 30 seconds, another may communicate the challenges of their least favorite class, and another spoke about the weather. Art can come from all sorts of surprising sources. Anything can be art. In this discussion, you can ask your students: "What makes something art?", an endlessly interesting topic.

Activity 3

Thinking About Themes

An analysis of song lyrics to explore techniques for thematic writing.

Time
30–45 minutes

Setting
Students should be seated in a circle facing each other.

Description
The students will examine the lyrics to the song chosen in Lesson 2 and determine how the lyrics create a consistent theme. Then they will juxtapose the lyrics with the instrumental to learn the sections of a song.

Exercise

- Students should be seated in a circle or cypher so they can all see each other.

- Hand out the lyrics to the song that was chosen the day before. Ask the students to read the lyrics, taking turns highlighting specific moments that they feel contribute to the song's consistent theme.

- Have the students share their findings with the class.

- Distribute copies of the "Songwriting Terms" handout that has been provided.

- Referring to the "Songwriting Terms" handout, introduce the students to the sections of a song: Introduction, Verse, Chorus, and Bridge. Always ask the students for suggestions on what to play and be aware of the rhythmic changes that occur with time. www.youtube.com and www.soundcloud.com are great resources. If the students feel stuck, feel free to offer up a

popular song. Discuss the structure of each section and how they commonly appear in a song.

- Now have the students analyze the lyrics to the song with the instrumental. (Note for playing instrumentals: you will need an internet connection or to download the instrumentals in advance. Always ask the students for suggestions on what to play and be aware of the rhythmic changes that occur with time. www.youtube.com and www.soundcloud.com are great resources. If you or your students have a phone or computer, you will need to connect the device to speakers via an 1/8" cable.)

- Ask the students: What are the sections of the song? How many bars is each section made up of? Note: "Bars" (also known as "measures") are a system for counting music. The majority of popular music is in the time signature of 4/4, which means there are 4 beats in every line of music. If you require a physical demonstration, search "How to count Bars" on YouTube.

- When the students have finished, initiate a discussion:

  ▸ How does the designation of specific sections of the song help the lyricist to create a theme?

  ▸ How does the instrumental coincide with the theme? i.e. "The hi-hats speed up during the chorus, where the lyrics talk about being happy."

- The students might decide that the lyrics do not articulate a consistent theme, or that the instrumental is not fitting to the lyrics. This is good, and shows that the students are carefully analyzing the material and formulating their own opinions.[4]

[4] Unit 1, Lesson 3 Common Core Alignment:
CCSS.ELA-LITERACY.CCRA.L.1–Demonstrate command of the conventions of standard English grammar and usage when writing or speaking.
CCSS.ELA-LITERACY.CCRA.L.3–Apply knowledge of language to understand how language functions in different contexts, to make effective choices for meaning or style, and to comprehend more fully when reading or listening.
CCSS.ELA-LITERACY.CCRA.L.4–Determine or clarify the meaning of unknown and multiple-meaning words and phrases by using context clues, analyzing meaningful word parts, and consulting general and specialized reference materials, as appropriate.
CCSS.ELA-LITERACY.CCRA.L.5–Demonstrate understanding of figurative language, word relationships, and nuances in word meanings.

CCSS.ELA-LITERACY.CCRA.L.6–Acquire and use accurately a range of general academic and domain-specific words and phrases sufficient for reading, writing, speaking, and listening at the college and career readiness level; demonstrate independence in gathering vocabulary knowledge when encountering an unknown term important to comprehension or expression.
CCSS.ELA-LITERACY.CCRA.SL.2–Integrate and evaluate information presented in diverse media and formats, including visually, quantitatively, and orally.
CCSS.ELA-LITERACY.CCRA.SL.3–Evaluate a speaker's point of view, reasoning, and use of evidence and rhetoric.
CCSS.ELA-LITERACY.CCRA.SL.5–Make strategic use of digital media and visual displays of data to express information and enhance understanding of presentations.
SMP 6–Attend to precision

HANDOUT
Songwriting Terms

Introduction
A unique musical passage meant to draw the listener into the song. For example, many Hip Hop producers start off a song with a quote meant to set the tone for the following lyrical material.

Pre-Chorus
A short passage meant to lead into the chorus. Especially in a context when the verses and chorus are on different energy levels, this songwriting device can be useful in making a smoother transition between sections.

Chorus
The chorus usually appears at least more than once throughout the course of the song, and often seeks to distill the subject of the verses into one phrase or stanza. The chorus is often the most distinguished part of the song, and serves to help the listener remember the song.

Verse
The verse carries the details, story, and other more in-depth material that the chorus attempts to distill. A typical song has 2 to 5 unique verses.

Bridge
The bridge is defined by its difference from the Chorus and Verses, and is usually used to break up the repetitive pattern of a song by using different harmonic, rhythmic, or melodic elements.

Solo
Section of a song open for an instrumentalist or vocalist to improvise over.

Outro
How will you end the song? This could be as simple as repeating the last line of the last verse, or as complex as using a new idea to hint at something more.

Lesson 4
Finesse The Pen

Suggested Time
45–60 minutes

Lesson 4 Overview
Lesson 4 consists of an acrostic poem activity in which students will write a short poem and recite it to the class, as well as a collaborative writing activity in which students will be broken up into groups and begin working on a group piece that they will perform in Lesson 5.

Activities

Activity 1
Acrostic Poems
Poetic writing activity

- Students will learn to recite a poem with emphasis and inflection

- Students will have their first chance to work on a written piece

Activity 2
Beginning A Song
Collaborative writing activity

- Students will collaborate on their first piece

- Introduction to Word Banks and Bubble Diagrams as writing techniques

Materials

- **Students:**
  - Beat Rhymers notebooks and writing utensils
- **Instructor**
  - Large writing surface with writing utensils
  - Large pieces of poster paper and markers to distribute to student groups
  - Music player (computer, iPhone, anything that can store and play music) and speakers

Activity 1

Acrostic Poems

A brief poetic writing activity.

Time
15–20 minutes

Setting
Class is split into even groups of 3-5 students each. The groups should be seated together, facing the teacher, and each student should have their notebook and a pencil out and be ready to write.

Tone
This should be an upbeat, fun activity. Keep it lively by encouraging the students to be themselves and be friendly with one another.

Description
Students will write acrostic poems based on their names, and will perform each other's poems for the rest of the group.

Exercise
- Instruct each student to write their name in big letters, vertically on one page of their notebook.

- Once this is done, give the class 10 minutes to come up with a poem where each line begins with one of the letters in their name.

- Example for a student named Tina:

  ▶ Towering, tall and talented

  ▶ I know who I am

  ▶ No one can take my identity away

  ▶ Anyone who tries will feel my wrath

- Each line can be as long or as short as the student wants.

- Once the 10 minutes is up, have each student in the group get into a small circle, and exchange poems with a partner

- For the last 5-10 minutes, each student will perform the poem they were given by their group member. However, they shouldn't introduce the name before performing. Through word emphasis, they should attempt to convey whose poem it is. They could pause between every line, or say the first word of each line with a similar inflection.

- After each performance, the group should guess whose poem it was.

Activity 2

Beginning A Song

Students will collaborate on their first piece.

Time
30–45 minutes

Setting
Class is randomly broken into groups of 3-5, seated together with a surface to write on.

Description
Students will be broken up into groups to collaborate on their first pieces. Each group member will contribute 4 bars of rhyming poetry, using Word Banks and Bubble Diagrams (which will be described inside the exercise) to help get them started.

Exercise
- Each group gets a piece of poster paper.

- Each group must create a team name.

- Next, the teacher should play a preselected instrumental on repeat. This could be a beat from a song the participants are aware of downloaded or an original compositions from a student, guest lecturer/musician, or you. Groups should clap along with it, and count the bars per musical section.

- Suggested Instrumentals:

  ▶ Tyga: "Rack City" Instrumental

  ▶ Taylor Swift ft. Kendrick Lamar: "Bad Blood" Instrumental

  ▶ Drake ft. Majid Jordan: "Hold On, We're Going Home" Instrumental

  ▶ J Dilla: "Thought U Wuz Nice" Instrumental

  ▶ Young Thug: "Check" Instrumental

- Each group should come up with an emotion or theme that they feel matches the instrumental. Once they decide on this, they write it down in the middle of the poster and circle it.

- At this point, introduce the writing concepts of the Word Bank and Bubble Diagram.

A Word Bank is a list of words that rhyme with each other.

  ▶ For example, it could look like: fat, cat, bat, sat, trap, etc.

A Bubble Diagram is a list of connected terms/themes/words that are arranged around the main theme and are connected by a web of lines and arrows. The main theme would be surrounded by a circle in the middle of the page, while the connected themes in boxes or circles of their own are connected to the main theme and each other with lines and/or arrows.

Each group should take a few minutes to write up a Bubble Diagram and Word Bank on their poster. Instructor should demonstrate an example with the students.

- Using the Word Bank and Bubble Diagram, each member of each group should come up with four bars of rhyming poetry. These lines can be simple in composition; the point is to introduce the concept of thematic writing rather than expect the students to write an award-winning verse.

- Within the group, everyone should participate in practicing and reciting their 4 lines.

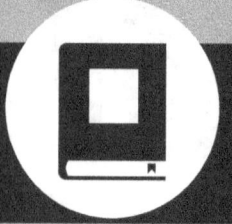

HOMEWORK

Students will revisit the bars they wrote in class. They can perfect their 4 bars or add on bars to make an 8 or 16 bar verse, or do both.

[5]Unit 1, Lesson 4 Common Core Alignment:
CCSS.ELA-LITERACY.CCRA.L.1—Demonstrate command of the conventions of standard English grammar and usage when writing or speaking.
CCSS.ELA-LITERACY.CCRA.L.2—Demonstrate command of the conventions of standard English capitalization, punctuation, and spelling when writing.
CCSS.ELA-LITERACY.CCRA.SL.1—Prepare for and participate effectively in a range of conversations and collaborations with diverse partners, building on others' ideas and expressing their own clearly and persuasively.
CCSS.ELA-LITERACY.CCRA.SL.6—Adapt speech to a variety of contexts and communicative tasks, demonstrating command of formal English when indicated or appropriate.
CCSS.ELA-LITERACY.CCRA.W.4—Produce clear and coherent writing in which the development, organization, and style are appropriate to task, purpose, and audience.
CCSS.ELA-LITERACY.CCRA.W.5—Develop and strengthen writing as needed by planning, revising, editing, rewriting, or trying a new approach.
CCSS.ELA-LITERACY.CCRA.W.10—Write routinely over extended time frames (time for research, reflection, and revision) and shorter time frames (a single sitting or a day or two) for a range of tasks, purposes, and audiences.
SMP 6—Attend to precision

Suggested Time

45–60 minutes

Lesson 5 Overview

Lesson 5 consists of a brief revision of the student's first collaborative piece, and its performance.

Activities

Activity 1

Step Up To The Stage

Performance of first collaborative piece

- Students will revise their songs

- Introduction to the concept of an intro and outro

- Students will gain performance experience

Materials

- **Students**
  - ▸ Beat Rhymers notebooks and writing utensils

- **Instructor**
  - ▸ Large writing surface with writing utensils

*Please note that students are never required to "Rap". They can always express themselves in any form of vocal expression whether that be singing, poetry, or prose. However, students should participate in all activities to build confidence and learn new skills while developing a basic musical foundation they can apply both to their art and to their lives.

Activity 1

Step Up To The Stage

Students will perform their first collaborative piece.

Time
45-60 minutes

Setting

Break students into their same groups from the last lesson, seated together with a surface to write on.

Description

Students will revise their first collaborative piece from Lesson 4 and develop an intro and outro to their performance. Then they will perform the piece for the class.

Exercise

- To begin, give them 10 minutes to share the revisions they made to their 4 bars with their group members, and to decide on the order of the verses.

- Once this time has passed, alert the groups that they must have some sort of preconceived intro and outro included in their performances.

- The intro must grab the audience's attention, and introduce the team.

- The outro must in some way introduce the next act.

- **Example**

- Intro: "Ladies and Gentlemen, we are the flying squirrels! 1, 2, 3, 4!"

  ▶ Outro: "Thank you thank you, we're out! Next up, the amazing Talking Juice Boxes! Give it up!"

- As a class, decide on an order of performances so that each team knows who is going on before and after them.

- Give the class 5 minutes to decide on and practice their intros and outros.

Performance Time

The students do not need to perform a rap or use the beat you played in class, unless they choose to do so. The goal is to allow them to feel comfortable expressing themselves in front of the group. Allow them to make this performance their own and make mistakes. Additionally, you do not need to expect them to memorize their verses, though it is encouraged. This is a great opportunity for you as an instructor to re-emphasize a collaborative, supportive, and safe environment.

Tone

Keep the atmosphere positive and respectful. Make sure students clap and show appreciation after every performance. Even if students make mistakes, emphasize that this is a learning environment, allow them to complete their performance and end with an outro. While these performances may take most of the class, do your best to leave 5-10 minutes at the end for reflection.

When the performances are finished, initiate a discussion:

- How was each performance different?

- What skills and strengths did different groups exhibit?

- What made an effective intro and outro?

- How did you feel during and after you performance?

After talking about what went well with the performance, let students know that they have finished Unit 1 of the Beat Rhymers class. Now is a good time to get feedback:

- "Those who feel they have a firm understanding of the material learned in lessons 1-5, give me a thumbs up. Those who feel they have an O.K. understanding of the material learned in lessons 1-5, give me a thumb sideways. Those who feel they do not understand the material learned in lessons 1-5, give me a thumbs down."

- "Those who feel they are comfortable expressing themselves in front of their fellow students, give me a thumbs up. Those who feel they are O.K. with expressing themselves in front of their fellow students, give me a thumb sideways. Those who feel they are not at all comfortable expressing themselves in front of their fellow students, give me a thumbs down."

- Record the students' responses to these questions.

- Feel free to create your own questions! Here are a few other examples:
  - "Who feels they are more comfortable expressing them in front of everyone now than when we first started?"
  - "Who feels that they have accomplished something?"

- Give positive reinforcement and remind them that we all grow at our own pace, and being nervous does not have to stop you! Acknowledge their courage and their process. Just the willingness to try something new is a major accomplishment.

Remember that the main purpose of Unit 1 is to ensure students feel comfortable with expressing themselves in front of each other. This is the most difficult but most essential obstacle to overcome before moving forward to Unit 2.

If more that 30% of the students do not understand the material, do not move on to Unit 2. Identify the areas the participants are having difficulty with and have the students that comprend teach the other participants.

- If more than 30% of the students do not feel comfortable expressing themselves in front of their fellow students, we recommend that you do not move on to Unit 2.

- The responses given by the class during your discussion can serve as a statistical survey of how many students understand the material and feel comfortable expressing themselves in front of their fellow students, but we also recommend that you use your judgement as an educator to gauge the development of the class and individual students. Keep in mind that students may not recognize their level of development or may not be willing to express when they do not comprehend something at this point in the class. When the participants have successfully embodied the objectives of these lessons, you are ready to move on to Unit 2.

[6]Unit 1, Lesson 5 Common Core Alignment:
CCSS.ELA-LITERACY.CCRA.W.3–Write narratives to develop real or imagined experiences or events using effective technique, well-chosen details and well-structured event sequences.
CCSS.ELA-LITERACY.CCRA.W.10–Write routinely over extended time frames (time for research, reflection, and revision) and shorter time frames (a single sitting or a day or two) for a range of tasks, purposes, and audiences.

CCSS.ELA-LITERACY.CCRA.SL.1–Prepare for and participate effectively in a range of conversations and collaborations with diverse partners, building on others' ideas and expressing their own clearly and persuasively.
CCSS.ELA-LITERACY.CCRA.SL.6–Adapt speech to a variety of contexts and communicative tasks, demonstrating command of formal English when indicated or appropriate
SMP 6–Attend to precision

WHAT WORKS
What lessons/activities did your class respond positively to?

STEPS FOR IMPROVEMENT
What lessons/activities need to be modified to be more effective?

_____ _____

_____ _____

_____ _____

_____ _____

_____ _____

_____ _____

_____ _____

_____ _____

_____ _____

_____ _____

_____ _____

_____ _____

_____ _____

_____ _____

_____ _____

_____ _____

_____ _____

_____ _____

NOTES
Any additional notes
you'd like to add
for this unit?

UNIT 2
FUNDAMENTALS: TOOLS OF THE TRADE

At this point the classroom has been established as a safe space and everyone is clear on the expectations for the course. This unit's purpose is to introduce them to the fundamentals of music. A firm understanding of these building blocks is paramount to the art of MCing. Each day of class will focus on one of four fundamentals:

Lesson 6: Basic Musicality

- Lesson 7: Writing
- Lesson 8: Improvisation
- Lesson 9: Performance Skills
- Lesson 10: On this day the students will perform for one another to show their grasp of the above four fundamentals.
- Students will use the skills they gain in Unit 2 in every subsequent unit, so it remains of vital importance that you not move on to Unit 3 until the majority of the class understands and can demonstrate the required knowledge. This course is mainly taught with the practice of Hip Hop music in mind. However, the tools provided in this unit are general enough to be applied to many other forms of creative expression. Our students have successfully participated in Beat Rhymers programs as singers, poets, producers, and instrumentalists. The purpose of this program and specifically this unit is to give students tools they can use to follow their own artistic paths. Not every student will connect with every activity the same way. Remind the students that every musician is familiar with all of the four fundamentals. Most activities can be molded and changed to fit the needs and interests of individuals.

Lesson 6
Back To The Basics

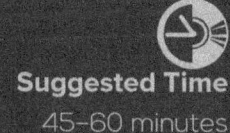

Suggested Time
45–60 minutes

Lesson 6 Overview
Lesson 6 consists of a discussion on the elements of basic musicality and an activity where students will use their bodies to make music.

Activities

Activity 1
The Basic Instinct

Discussion

Students will understand tempo, rhythm, melody, and dynamics

Activity 2
Human Orchestra

Making music

- Students will use the concepts of tempo, rhythm, melody, and dynamics to make music

- Students will learn about looping, performance, and collaboration

Materials

- **Students**
  - ▶ Beat Rhymers notebooks and writing utensils
- **Instructor**
  - ▶ Large writing surface with writing utensils
  - ▶ Print out copies of the "Note Duration" handout provided at the end of the lesson.

Activity 1

The Basic Instinct

Exploring the basic elements of music.

Time
25–30 minutes

Setting
Students should be seated facing the large writing surface on which you will be taking notes.

Description
Students will be introduced to the elements of basic musicality: Tempo, Rhythm, Melody, and Dynamics. Students will also be introduced to common tempos (BPMs) across different styles of music and note duration. This section is designed to give all participants a basic understanding of music fundamentals, and will be essential for any students looking to rap, sing, produce or play an instrument as part of the course. This can also be a great point to bring in a guest musician to teach this if you do not feel comfortable doing so.

Exercise

- Write these definitions on the large writing surface:

  ▶ Tempo (BPM): the number of beats per minute in a piece of music

  ▶ Rhythm: the arrangement of sounds as they move through time.

  ▶ Melody: a rhythmical succession of tones producing a distinct musical phrase or idea.

  ▶ Dynamics: The qualities of a sound or musical phrase (soft, loud, fast, slow, etc.).

The students do not need to know these definitions by heart. In fact, we do not believe it is required that you teach these definitions as a part of your curriculum. We believe that music is best taught when it is made. Your students already understand tempo, rhythm, melody, and dynamics. They may not know it, but they have embodied these concepts in activities like Shabooya, Two Bars and Pass, and their collaborative performance. This is the only real knowledge they need to execute musicality in the creative process. With that said, clearly defining these concepts for the students can't hurt. Allow the students to choose if they would like to know the technical definitions , we strongly suggest that you do not let them take

precedence over the actual act of creating music. If a student cannot recite the definition for tempo from memory, but can clap a consistent tempo, they are more than prepared for the rest of the class.

Though we maintain that the above definitions are not required, we do recommend that you expose your students to common tempos across popular genres of music and note duration. See the handout attached at the end of this lesson. Whether or not you choose to define and discuss these concepts with your students, they will be fully embodied in the next activities.

Activity 2

Human Orchestra

Students will use the sound of their bodies to create live music.

Time
25–30 minutes

Setting
Everyone standing in a circle facing inwards so that you are visible to one another.

Tone
Keep students active and engaged by using question based prompts such as: "Who can tell me what tempo is?". Allow students to answer first, then chime in after to build on their responses, whether correct or not. Do not overemphasize technical definitions, leave room for the youth to converse and teach each other.

Description
The instructor introduces his or her self as the "conductor" and provides a tempo. Each member of the class contributes a sound they repeat in time with the tempo. The sound can be anything from a clap, words, to a whistle. The students will receive the opportunity to play the "conductor", which includes the ability to silence individuals, make them louder/ quieter, and speed up or slow down the group creating variations in the loop. These changes occur through specific hand motions or gestures that you can create on your own or with your students.

Exercise

- To begin, create a steady tempo, clapping on the "2 and 4" counts of each bar. (1 2 3 4)
- While students are clapping, explain that each

student, going around the circle, must create a rhythm and sound to add to the "human orchestra." For example, it could be as simple as saying "yo" on beat 4 of every bar.

- Once there are a few students participating, drop out the clapping to see if they can hold the tempo without the claps. Students will be adding their own unique words and sounds.

- After a few more students add their rhythms and sounds, introduce the role of the "conductor," someone who stands in the middle and controls the loops. Establish a motion that signifies On/Off (ex: open hand = On, closed hand = Off), and one for Softer/Louder (ex: lowering hand towards the ground = Softer, raising hand towards the sky = Louder). After demonstrating a few times, allow a student to take your place.

- If students begin to get off time, have the conductor "solo" out one of the sounds (meaning mute all students but one), and have everyone start from scratch again.

After several conductors have gone, initiate a discussion:

- What did we learn about looping?
- What did we learn about performance?
- What did we learn about collaboration?

Exercise

- What we did as a large group, we'll now do on a smaller scale. Have each group make a loop of 16 bars, split into two different 8 bar variations. Each 8 bars should be rhythmically different than the other, and should also contain different sounds.

- Here, you can distribute the "Note Duration" handout for reference. Remind your students that they do not need to memorize this, but it can be helpful in constructing their 8 bar variations.

- A simple example: 8 bars of claps on all four beats, followed by 8 bars of snaps just on the "3."

- Once each group has established their loop sequences, have two groups come up to the front, form two lines and stand facing one another. One of the groups will start their loop, and it is the job of the other group to mimic them. Each student should be replicating the sounds and rhythms of the student across from them.

- You can again "solo" out a pair of students to make sure they're doing the same thing, or use any of the other conductor commands used in the previous lesson.

Extension Activity

 Time
25–30 minutes

Setting
Students split into groups of 3-5, each group in a circle.

Description
Students will split into groups of 3-5 and create a loop like in Activity 1 with their group members. The groups will then meet to try and replicate each other's loop.

Unit 2, Lesson 6 Common Core Alignment:
z- Acquire and use accurately a range of general academic and domain-specific words and phrases sufficient for reading, writing, speaking, and listening at the college and career readiness level; demonstrate independence in gathering vocabulary knowledge when encountering an unknown term important to comprehension or expression.
CCSS.ELA-LITERACY.CCRA.W.10–Write routinely over extended time frames (time for research, reflection, and revision) and shorter time frames (a single sitting or a day or two) for a range of tasks, purposes, and audiences.
CCSS.ELA-LITERACY.CCRA.SL.2–Integrate and evaluate information presented in diverse media and formats, including visually, quantitatively, and orally.
SMP 2 – Reason abstractly and quantitatively
SMP 4 – Model with mathematics
SMP 5 – Use appropriate tools strategically

HANDOUT
Note Duration

In 4/4 time, each bar is broken down into 4 beats. The way that musicians normally measure the length of a note or rhythmic element is to denote how much space within a bar this note or element takes up. You can use this chart to create and teach basic rhythm without words using stomps, claps or sounds if needed.

 A whole note takes up the whole bar (4 beats)

 A half note takes up half the bar (2 beats)

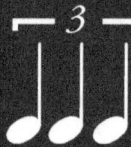 A quarter note triplet, also takes up half the bar (2 beats), but is subdivided into three separate notes

 A quarter note takes up a quarter of the bar (1 beat)

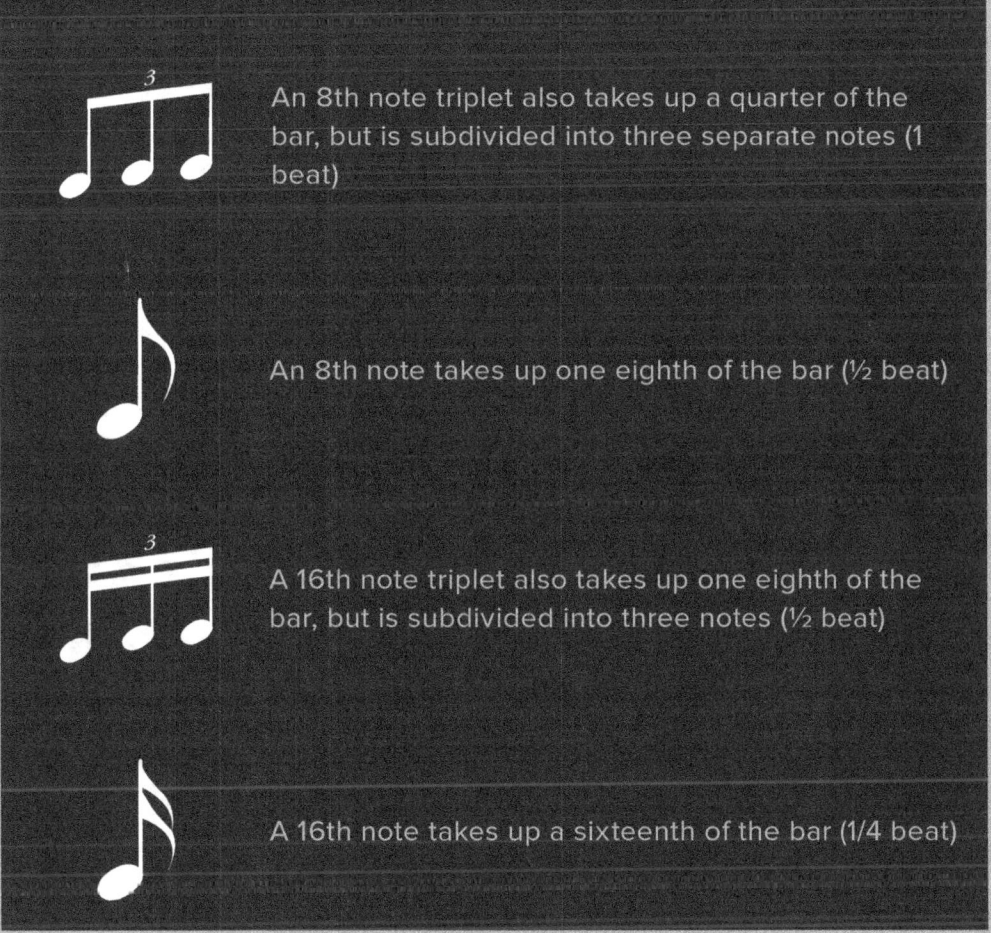

An 8th note triplet also takes up a quarter of the bar, but is subdivided into three separate notes (1 beat)

An 8th note takes up one eighth of the bar (½ beat)

A 16th note triplet also takes up one eighth of the bar, but is subdivided into three notes (½ beat)

A 16th note takes up a sixteenth of the bar (1/4 beat)

Lesson 7
Sharpen Your Lyrical Blade

Lesson 7 Overview

Lesson 7 consists of a discussion on literary devices and how they can be used in the writing process as well as an activity using those literary devices to write a piece.

Activities

Activity 1
The Pad and the Pen

Discussion

- Students will explore the most common literary devices

Activity 2
Story Time

Group story-writing

- Students will use literary devices to write a story

Materials

- **Students**
  - ▸ Beat Rhymers notebooks and writing utensils
- **Instructor**
  - ▸ Large writing surface with writing utensils
  - ▸ Print out of "Literary Devices" handout

Activity 1

The Pad and the Pen

Exploring literary devices that can be used to write lyrics.

Time
15–20 minutes

Setting
Students should be seated facing the large writing surface while you take notes on it.

Description
Students should be given the handout (see end of this lesson plan) with 7 literary devices and use it to write a 4 bar piece. For an expansive list of literary devices, please visit www.literary-devices.com.

Exercise

- Begin with the question: "What can we do to make our writing better?"

"We can learn how to use literary devices to give our writing a more interesting structure."

- "Here are 5 of the most common literary devices..." [write the following definitions on the large writing space]:

  ▶ Metaphor: a meaning or identity ascribed to one subject by way of another

    • Example: "We rock the house like rock 'n roll, got more soul than a sock with a hole, set the stage with a goal, to have the game locked in a cage getting shocked with a pole."–MF Doom on "Rhinestone Cowboy", Madvillainy

  ▶ Simile: drawing parallels or comparisons between two unrelated and dissimilar things, people, beings, places, and concepts

    • Example: "My rhymes are like shot clocks, interstate cops and blood clots, my point is your flow gets stopped."–Talib Kweli on "Hater Players", Mos Def and Talib Kweli Are Blackstar

    • Alliteration: words are used in quick succession and begin with letters belonging to the same sound group

    • Example: "Artificial amateurs, aren't at all amazing analytically, I assault, animate things, broken barriers bounded by the bomb beat, buildings are broken, basically I'm bombarding."–Gift of Gab on "Alphabet Aerobics", A2G

  ▶ Imagery: uses words and phrases to create "mental images"

  ▶ Example: "Yo, weeks went by and I'm surprised, Still stuck in the shelf with all the things that an outlaw hides, besides me it's bullets, two vests and then a nine, there's a grenade in a box, and that tech that kept cryin' cause he ain't been cleaned in a year, he's rusty as clear he's 'bout to fall to pieces, cause of his murder career."–Nas on "I Gave You Power", It Was Written

  ▶ Onomatopoeia: words whose very sound is very close to the sound they are meant to depict

    • Example: Can I get some fries with that shake-shake boobie? If looks could kill you would be an uzi, You're a shotgun–bang! What's up with that thang?–Salt n' Peppa on "Shoop"

- These are 5 of the most popular literary devices, and the ones most commonly used in a rapper's lyrical playbook, but there exist many more. Distribute the "Literary Devices" handout to your students now, which has 7 examples. If your students know any more literary devices, encourage them to share and add them to the class list. An exhaustive list of literary devices can be found on literary-devices.com.

- As with the definitions we gave in Lesson 6, the definitions represented here do not need to be memorized, and the entire list of literary devices does not need to be explored for your students to have the tools to write profound poetry. Your purpose here is to get the students thinking about what makes a unique and expressive poem/rap. They do not need to memorize the definitions of the literary devices (there is much more to rap than lyrical complexity, after all). Yet they can serve as kickstarters to help get the writing process moving.

- Have the students use at least one of the 5 literary devices to write 4 bars of poetry.

- Allow some time at the end for students to share their poetry with the rest of the class. This can be done with a beat playing or acapella, depending on what your students want.

Activity 2

Story Time

Telling a story with literary devices.

Time
30–40 minutes

Setting
Class is split into even groups of 3-5 students each. The groups should be seated together, facing the teacher, and each student should have their notebook and a pencil out and be ready to write.

Description
Each group will write a short story using literary devices.

Exercise

- Each student writes 4 lines of poetry.

- Each one of the 4 lines of poetry should use at least one of the 5 literary devices provided in Activity 1.

Note: Students can and should use other devices than the ones provided if they know them.

Each poem should tell a story.

- Let the students work it out themselves. Walk around as they're working, offer advice, and listen to their issues.

- Be sure to analyze each group's submissions and provide constructive feedback when necessary.[9]

Extension Activity

Time
25–30 minutes

Setting
Students seated facing the teacher.

Description
Choose a song that the class likes and analyze its use of literary devices.

Exercise

Have the class vote on a song they would like to analyze

Give the students access to the lyrics. Analyze each line as a class.

Have the students raise their hands and call out literary devices they find in each line.

Unit 2, Lesson 7 Common Core Alignment:

CCSS.ELA-LITERACY.CCRA.R.4–Interpret words and phrases as they are used in a text, including determining technical, connotative, and figurative meanings, and analyze how specific word choices shape meaning or tone.

CCSS.ELA-LITERACY.CCRA.W.10–Write routinely over extended time frames (time for research, reflection, and revision) and shorter time frames (a single sitting or a day or two) for a range of tasks, purposes, and audiences.

CCSS.ELA-LITERACY.CCRA.L.3–Apply knowledge of language to understand how language functions in different contexts, to make effective choices for meaning or style, and to comprehend more fully when reading or listening.

CCSS.ELA-LITERACY.CCRA.L.5–Demonstrate understanding of figurative language, word relationships, and nuances in word meanings.

CCSS.ELA-LITERACY.CCRA.W.3–Write narratives to develop real or imagined experiences or events using effective technique, well-chosen details and well-structured event sequences.

SMP 6 – Attend to precision

SMP 7 – Look for and make use of structure

SMP 8 – Look for and express regularity in repeated reasoning

Handout
Literary Devices

Below are the seven most commonly used literary devices that can be used to enhance any piece of writing, along with examples from popular Hip Hop songs. Where are the literary device in each example? How can you use these in your written pieces? In your daily life? (For a comprehensive list of literary devices, please visit www. literary-devices.com)

Metaphor

A meaning or identity ascribed to one subject by way of another

Example: "We rock the house like rock 'n roll, got more soul than a sock with a hole, set the stage with a goal, to have the game locked in a cage getting shocked with a pole." – MF Doom on "Rhinestone Cowboy", Madvillainy

Simile

Drawing parallels or comparisons between two unrelated and dissimilar things, people, beings, places, and concepts

Example: "My rhymes are like shot clocks, interstate cops and blood clots, my point is your flow gets stopped."   Talib Kweli on "Hater Players", Mos Def and Talib Kweli Are Blackstar

Alliteration

Words are used in quick succession and begin with letters belonging to the same sound group

- Example: "Artificial amateurs, aren't at all amazing analytically, I assault, animate things, broken barriers bounded by the bomb beat, buildings are broken, basically I'm bombarding." – Gift of Gab on "Alphabet Aerobics", A2G

Imagery

Uses words and phrases to create "mental images"

Example: "Yo, weeks went by and I'm surprised, Still stuck in the shelf with all the things that an outlaw hides, besides me it's bullets, two vests and then a nine, there's a grenade in a box, and that tech that kept cryin' cause he ain't been cleaned in a year, he's rusty as clear he's 'bout to fall to pieces, cause of his murder career." – Nas on "I Gave You Power", It Was Written

Onomatopoeia

Words whose very sound is very close to the sound they are meant to depict

- Example: "Can I get some fries with that shake-shake boobie? If looks could kill you would be an uzi, You're a shotgun—bang! What's up with that thang?" — Salt n' Peppa on "Shoop", Very Necessary

Allusion

A figure of speech whereby the author refers to a subject matter such as a place, event, or literary work by way of a passing reference. It is up to the reader to make a connection to the subject being mentioned.

- Example: "Stock markets just crash, now I'm just a bill, History don't repeat itself, it rhymes, 1929, still, Write like Mark Twain, Jay Gatsby, I park things, Yellow cars, yellow gold..." — Jay Z on "100$ Bill", Great Gatsby Soundtrack

Rhyme Scheme

The practice of rhyming words placed at the end of the lines in the prose or poetry. Rhyme scheme refers to the order in which particular words rhyme. If the alternate words rhyme, it is an "a-b-a-b" rhyme scheme, which means "a" is the rhyme for the lines 1 and 3 and "b" is the rhyme affected in the lines 2 and 4.

- Example: "Bust rap tunes on flat spoons, Take no shorts like poom pooms, See hoochies pop coochies, for Gucci's and Lucci, Find me in my Mitsubishi, eatin' sushi, bumpin' Fugees." — Lauryn Hill on The Fugees "Fu-Gee-La", The Score

- What is the rhyme scheme in the above example?

- What other literary devices do you know?

- What are some of your favorite musical examples of literary devices in use?

Freestyle Fellowship

Suggested Time
45–60 minutes

Lesson 8 Overview

Lesson 8 consists of a word association activity and a guess-the-word activity, each to help the students generate ideas for performance using improvisation.

Activities

Activity 1
The Pad and the Pen

Discussion

Students will explore the most common literary devices

Activity 2
Story Time

Group story-writing

Students will use literary devices to write a story

Materials

- **Students**
  - ▶ Beat Rhymers notebooks and writing utensils
- **Instructor**
  - ▶ Large writing surface with writing utensils
  - ▶ A hat, bowl, or any container big enough to hold a dozen slips of paper

Activity 1

Word Association

An improvisational activity combining words and motions.

Time
30–45 minutes

Setting
Everyone stands in a circle facing inwards

Tone
This should be an upbeat, fun activity. Keep it lively by encouraging students to be themselves and be friendly with one another.

Description
Students will play an improvisational game of word association in which specific directed motions are linked to different trains of thought. This activity is useful as it combines improvisation with group cooperation and songwriting technique.

Exercise

- Start by introducing a range of numbers and a direction around the circle. Ask the students to "pass the pattern" while miming a gesture.

- Example: I would turn left to Pablo and say "One!" while making a pushing movement. Pablo would turn left to Sally and say "Two!" while making the same motion." This goes until the number cap, say 5, is reached, and the cypher starts over at 1.

- Next, ask the students to go the opposite way (facing right), this time reciting letters and miming a different gesture. When this is complete, repeat the same process as above, this time using letters and going in the opposite direction with a new motion. When the students are comfortable with moving in both directions, ask them to switch it up between one direction with numbers and the other with letters.

- The purpose of this is to associate the continuation of an idea or theme with a certain direction and motion. The actual activity begins when students take this idea of thematic continuity or discontinuity, and apply it to storytelling or writing.

- When the students are comfortable with this structure, move the focus of the game to word association. One direction of the circle starts with a word. Those who follow must choose a different word following the same train of thought. If a student wants to recite a word that is not in some way associated with the previous word, they must change the direction.

  ▶ Example: I turn left to Pablo and say "Sky!" while making a pushing movement. Pablo would turn let to Sally and say "Cloud!" while making the same motion. Sally might decide to change the subject of the word, so she would go in the opposite direction and introduce a new motion. She would turn to the right, back to Pablo, and say "Pizza!" while making a bowing motion.

- Now, take this a step further to tell a story. One person starts with a word, or even a phrase. The following person could either choose to build off of this and pass it along in the same direction, or change the path or theme of the story and make up a new motion, sending it back the other way around the circle.

After you have gone around the circle several times, or your story has ended,initiate a discussion:

- How can this game help us learn how to write lyrics?

  ▶ "Improvisation is a very important tool for writing lyrics. Improvisational writing allows us to capture a feeling or emotion in the moment. Even when writing lyrics, we should keep in mind improvisation and how it allows us to bring our current feelings into a piece."

  ▶ "In the next activity we will explore how improvisation is useful in conveying your current feelings to an audience during a performance."

Activity 2

Guess the Word

An improvisational activity to help the class guess a randomly chosen word.

Time
30–45 minutes

Setting
Everyone standing in a circle facing inwards so that you are visible to one another.

Description
Choose a word out of a hat. An individual will

perform some kind of improvisation until the class can guess what the word is.

Exercise

- Distribute a piece of paper to each student, collectively choose a topic, and ask them to write a relevant word on it. Students can also write random words if they choose. Collect the papers and mix them in a hat or other container.

- Each student will randomly select a paper when it is their turn and stand in the middle of the circle.

- The student in the middle of the circle will improvise, reciting words or motions that might indicate the word on their paper to the class without saying the actual word for 30-60 seconds.

- The class must guess the word on the student's paper based on their improvisation.

After everyone in the circle has gone, initiate a discussion:

- How is this activity useful for performance?

  ▶ "Being able to use improvisation to indicate something to the audience is a good skill to have. A good performer can use this skill to influence the audience's actions, making them stand-up, clap, repeat words, or dance. This skill allows you to control the energy of the audience during a performance."[10]

[10]Unit 2, Lesson 8 Common Core Alignment:
CCSS.ELA-LITERACY.CCRA.SL.1–Prepare for and participate effectively in a range of conversations and collaborations with diverse partners, building on others' ideas and expressing their own clearly and persuasively.
CCSS.ELA-LITERACY.CCRA.SL.6–Adapt speech to a variety of contexts and communicative tasks, demonstrating command of formal English when indicated or appropriate.
SMP 6–Attend to precision

Lesson 9
Craft Your Sound

Suggested Time
45–60 minutes

Lesson 9 Overview
Lesson 9 consists of a "Wall of Sound" activity to teach students about vocal projection, dynamics, and a performance activity to demonstrate the importance of body language.

Activities

Activity 1
Wall of Sound

Vocal projection activity

Students will become aware of the importance of projection in a performance

Activity 2
Human Machine

Body language exercise

Students will become aware of the importance of body language in a performance

Materials

- **Students**
  - ▶ Beat Rhymers notebooks and writing utensils
- **Instructor**
  - ▶ Large writing surface with writing utensils

Activity 1

Wall of Sound

A vocal projection activity.

Time
30–45 minutes

Setting
One student stands at the front of the class with area cleared while the others stand in the back.

Tone
This should be an upbeat, fun activity. Keep it lively by encouraging the students to be themselves and be friendly with one another.

Description
An individual stands at the front of the class and performs while the rest of the class stands at the back. The students standing in the back should slowly move towards the performer as soon as they have trouble hearing them.

Exercise

- Start the class by initiating a discussion:
  - ▶ What makes for a memorable performance?
  - ▶ Which performers have you seen who made an impression on you?
- What specifically in their performance spoke to you?
- Follow up this discussion by moving right into the activity.
- The student at the front of the class should begin by reciting something. Encourage students to recite original pieces. They can also improvise or you can provide short pieces of poetry or prose to read.
- Stand in the back of the class with the other students while each individual performs.
- If the students standing in the back of the class have trouble hearing the individual performing, they must slowly walk forward towards the front of the class and the performer.
- The individual at the front of the class must speak louder to push the other students back. If students walking towards the front of the room begin to hear the speaker, they must walk towards the back of the room.
- After every student has participated in the "Wall of Sound" initiate another discussion:

- What did the "Wall of Sound" teach you about the importance of vocal projection?
  - ▶ "The wall of sound activity requires you to project your vocals, regardless of what kind of material you are performing. In a vocal performance, the most important thing is that the audience can hear you. If the audience can't hear your voice, it doesn't matter how impressive your lyrics or flow are."

Activity 2

Human Machine

An exercise in body language.

Time
30–45 minutes

Setting
Class is split into even groups of 3-5 students each. The groups should be standing and ready to perform.

Tone
This should be an upbeat, fun activity. Keep it lively by encouraging the students to be themselves and be friendly with one another.

Description
The students will use their bodies to construct a "machine" that performs a certain task. Each member of the group will mime a certain movement that shows they are a part of an assembly line producing an imaginary product.

Exercise

- Have the groups organize into single file lines.
- Each group member should perform an improvised movement of any kind (optionally accompanied by a sound).
- They should start in order with the first group member, which leads into the next.
- Their movements should mimic "producing" an imaginary object, as an industrial machine does.
- When the object reaches the final member of the machine, that student should "present" the finished object, and the machine starts over.
- Eventually, the human machine will appear to be moving fluidly.

● Example

▶ The first student mimes the creation of a box-shaped object, and hands it down the line.

▶ The next student takes this "box" and crushes it into a smaller or different shape.

▶ The final student, upon receiving this changed object, will stretch it out and make a "ding!" sound to show that the process is complete.

▶ Repeat.

▶ When the students have clearly grasped the human machine concept, initiate a discussion:

▶ What does this activity teach us about the importance of body language?

- "The human machine activity requires you to use your body language to create the image of a moving machine. As you have seen, the more animated your body language, the more fluid the machine appears to be moving. Body language in a performance is as important as the integrity of your art. If your body language suggests that you are confident, the crowd will be more inclined to trust your proficiency as a performer. Your body language brings a visual element to musical performance, one that makes your performance more exciting and alive to the audience." [11]

Unit 2, Lesson 9 Common Core Alignment:
CCSS.ELA-LITERACY.CCRA.SL.1—Prepare for and participate effectively in a range of conversations and collaborations with diverse partners, building on others' ideas and expressing their own clearly and persuasively.
CCSS.ELA-LITERACY.CCRA.SL.2—Integrate and evaluate information presented in diverse media and formats, including visually, quantitatively, and orally.
SMP 1—Make sense of problems and persevere in solving them
SMP 6—Attend to precision.

Show and Prove

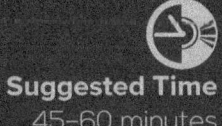

Suggested Time
45–60 minutes

Lesson 10 Overview
Lesson 10 consists of a skill-based performance by each student, followed by a discussion on the material learned in Unit 2.

Activities

Activity 1
Show and Prove
Performance activity

- Students will demonstrate what they've learned about music fundamentals

- Students become more comfortable expressing themselves in front of the class

Activity 2
What Makes A Team?
Discussion

Students will prepare for Unit 3.

- Staff will become more familiar with students' skills and interests

- Staff will gain information to organize students into groups for Unit 3

Materials

- **Students**
  - Beat Rhymers notebooks and writing utensils
- **Instructor**
  - Large writing surface with writing utensils

Activity 1

Show and Prove

A performance activity.

Time
Time: 30–40 minutes

Setting
Everyone standing in a circle facing inwards so that you are visible to one another.

Tone
This should be an upbeat, fun activity. Keep it lively by encouraging the students to be themselves and be friendly with one another.

Description
The students will demonstrate a musical skill they have learned during this unit.

Exercise

- Begin by initiating a discussion:

- What are the 4 fundamentals we learned in Unit 2? (Allow your students to discuss freely without correction, before adding on to be sure these 4 are understood):

  1. Basic Musicality

  2. Writing

  3. Improvisation

  4. Performance Skills

  ▶ What is something you learned in each lesson that helped you understand one of the four fundamentals?

- Have each student stand in the center of the circle and and demonstrate something that helped them understand one of the four fundamentals.

  ▶ (Their contribution doesn't need to be long or complex; a student might demonstrate they understand 8th notes by clapping for 4 bars. The point is to get students thinking about what they know coming out of Unit 2 that they didn't know when they started.(Next student goes, and so on)

  ▶ Once they've performed, write their name on the large writing surface next to the skill they performed. Ex: "Johnny: Counting"

  ▶ After everyone's gone, clap it up! Everyone's made strides since the first class.

Activity 2

What Makes A Team?

A precursor discussion for Unit 3.

Time
15–20 minutes

Setting
Students should be seated facing the large writing surface while you take notes on it.

Description
This activity is meant to serve as a precursor discussion to the next unit, which centers around collaboration.

Exercise

- Discussion Questions

  ▶ What are some of your favorite groups/teams/bands?

    • To facilitate discussion, mention that in a good group, each member compliments the whole. For a group to work effectively, each member must work to their strengths, and each member usually has a different strength.

    • Ask each student what they think their strengths are. Ask them what their interests, goals, and areas of improvement in the class are. Write each interest or goal down next to their names on the large piece of chart paper.

  ▶ Example: Johnny: Counting; Yolanda: Writing Songs; Jackson: Hype Man, etc.

  ▶ This information will be used to help you organize the students into groups for Unit 3.

  ▶ Finally, announce to your class that in the following unit, they will begin songwriting in earnest, and will have to make musical choices. One of these is whether they want to rap, sing, or do spoken word. As you will have seen, the lessons are leaning towards a more musical approach to songwriting. However, if a student feels like they want to do something poetic that does not contain rhythmic or melodic elements, this should be allowed on the condition that they still cultivate an understanding of the musical elements taught in the class (they should be able to count bars, know the basic note durations, etc.).

[12] Unit 2, Lesson 10 Common Core Alignment:
CCSS.ELA-LITERACY.CCRA.SL.1–Prepare for and participate effectively in a range of conversations and collaborations with diverse partners, building on others' ideas and expressing their own clearly and persuasively.
CCSS.ELA-LITERACY.CCRA.L.6–Acquire and use accurately a range of general academic and domain-specific words and phrases sufficient for reading, writing, speaking, and listening at the **SMP 7** – Look for and make use of structure college and career readiness level; demonstrate independence in gathering vocabulary knowledge when encountering an unknown term important to comprehension or expression.
SMP 1–Make sense of problems and persevere in solving them
SMP 3–Construct viable arguments and critique the reasoning of others

WHAT WORKS
What lessons/activities did your class respond positively to?

STEPS FOR IMPROVEMENT
What lessons/activities need to be modified to be more effective?

_____ _____

_____ _____

_____ _____

_____ _____

_____ _____

_____ _____

_____ _____

_____ _____

_____ _____

_____ _____

_____ _____

_____ _____

_____ _____

_____ _____

_____ _____

_____ _____

_____ _____

_____ _____

_____ _____

_____ _____

NOTES
Any additional notes you'd like to add for this unit?

_____

_____

_____

_____

_____

_____

_____

_____

_____

_____

_____

_____

_____

_____

_____

_____

_____

_____

_____

_____

_____

UNIT 3
COLLABORATION: LET'S FLIP THIS

The main purpose of this unit is to foster collaborative skills in students. By this point in the curriculum, students should be comfortable enough with one another that this goes relatively smoothly. If you think that such activities would still remain a challenge for the majority of your class, it is recommended that you revisit activities listed in previous lessons that you believe would best strengthen the collaborative nature of your class. This unit is also designed to act as a stepping stone towards individual songwriting. In working with their groups over a series of class periods, students will be able to experience the entire process, from brainstorming to performing, without having to do all of the creative work themselves. As you formulate the groups that will last for these five lessons, attempt to balance them out in terms of skill-set. If there are a few students who are advanced at writing or performing, spread them out into different groups. If there are students who bring other skills, like instrumentalism, MCing, beatboxing, beatmaking, comedy, or anything else that could be incorporated into performance, spread them out as well. Remember, you are here to facilitate the growth of your young people. If they want to add something to their performance and you feel that it's appropriate, let them.

Lesson 11
Form To Transform

Suggested Time
45-60 minutes

Lesson 11 Overview

Lesson 11 consists of a group formation activity to establish the groups for the rest of Unit 3. Groups will begin discussing the piece they would like to work on and present at the end of the Unit.

Activities 〰

Activity 1
Forming the Squad

Group formation activity

● Students will be placed into groups of 3-5 based on their strengths and interests

Activity 2
Squads Assemble

Brainstorming

● Groups will identify topics and elements of performance for their pieces

● Students will define their individual contributions to their group's piece

Materials

● **Students**

▶ Beat Rhymers notebooks and writing utensils

● **Instructor**

▶ Large writing surface with writing utensils

Activity 1

Forming The Squad

Students will be organized into their groups for the rest of the unit.

Time
Time: 20-35 minutes

Setting

Students should be seated facing the large writing surface while you take notes on it.

Tone

This should be an upbeat, fun activity. Keep it lively by encouraging the students to be themselves and be friendly with one another.

Description

Students will be split into their collaborative groups, which will last the entire unit.

Exercise

To start the class, you should recreate the list that you made in Lesson 10 of each student's strengths and interests. Coming into Lesson 11, you should have your own list of groups depending on what you know about each student and their strengths. However, we highly recommend that you allow the students to form their own groups. Being able to form a group is the first skill necessary to effectively collaborate. You can let the students know your recommendations for the groups, and if there is a group arrangement that you strongly disagree with you can move the students around. Encourage the students to form groups that are well-rounded and have multiple skillsets represented.

- Announce to the class that today they will be split into their groups for the remainder of the unit.

- Allow the students to collaborate in forming their own groups based on the list of skillsets you wrote on the large writing surface.

- Show the students your list for the groups and suggest that they start from there.

- It's very important that you hear the students out if they have an issue with one of the groups that you made. If it's just a matter of friends wanting to be with friends, keep the groups as they are. Remind them that these aren't lifelong groups, they'll just last for a few class periods.

- Note: In most Beat Rhymers classes, the collaborative piece takes the form of a rap song. Students select an instrumental and rhyme in time with it to create their song or use an instrumental produced by one of their fellow students. Remember, Beat Rhymers is about allowing students to express themselves. The collaborative piece does not have to be a rap. We only recommend that you require your students to perform something that is vocal; they can rap, recite poetry, or sing. The fundamentals that you have taught thus far are applicable to any of these forms of expression.

Activity 2

Squads Assemble

A period for the groups to get together and begin brainstorming

Time
25–35 minutes

Setting
Have newly formed groups get together and form little circles.

Description
Groups will begin to brainstorm the topic of their piece, as well as the elements of performance that will go into it.

Exercise

- The groups should use their papers and pencils to record their material.

- Each group should:
  - Come up with a group name.
  - Decide on a topic that they all have a common interest in. For example, if they are all from different neighborhoods and are all interested in repping their home, the common topic could be "Where I'm From."
  - Set individual goals for themselves within the context of their group. For example, " I want to write a verse," or "I want to write a catchy hook."
  - Each group will come up to the front and share their group names, topics, and individual goals.

- ▸ After every group has shared their group name, topic, and individual goals, initiate a discussion:

- ▸ What more is there to executing a musical performance other than just reciting your music?

  - • Memorization: "Before a performance, you must memorize your material and have enough of a grasp over it so that you can make it your own on stage."

  - • Stage Presence: "Your stage presence is determined by your body language, your projection, your confidence, and your appearance. Do you move around the stage like a dancer? Do you dress in a particular way?"

  - • Discuss rappers or performers that you or your students have seen who have a unique and engaging stage presence.

- • Ad-Libs: "Ad-Libs are small vocal improvisations you add to a performance. For example, between the verse and the chorus you might shout 'Here we go!' or 'Throw your hands up!'."

  - • Hype-Man: "As a rapper you might have a hype man in a performance, who stands on stage with you and gets the crowd moving or adds different ad-libs. The Hype-Man might introduce you to the crowd or echo lyrics that you rap."

- • Note: For the final performance, students will be asked to either make a new song or revisit one that they've already made in this course. Because they will compose and perform multiple songs throughout these five units, record all the group or individual performances so that when it comes time for students to look back on what they've done, you will have a definitive list for them to refer to.

HOMEWORK

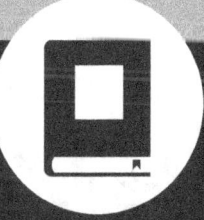

Students will do a 10 minute free write on their group's topic and bring these completed assignments in to the next class.[13]

[13] Unit 3, Lesson 11 Common Core Alignment:
CCSS.ELA-LITERACY.CCRA.W.5—Develop and strengthen writing as needed by planning, revising, editing, rewriting, or trying a new approach.
CCSS.ELA-LITERACY.CCRA.SL.1—Prepare for and participate effectively in a range of conversations and collaborations with diverse partners, building on others' ideas and expressing their own clearly and persuasively.
CCSS.ELA-LITERACY.CCRA.L.6—Acquire and use accurately a range of general academic and domain-specific words and phrases sufficient for reading, writing, speaking, and listening at the college and career readiness level; demonstrate independence in gathering vocabulary knowledge when encountering an unknown term important to comprehension or expression.
SMP 3 – Construct viable arguments and critique the reasoning of others
SMP 8 – Look for and express regularity in repeated reasoning

Lesson 12
Breaking Down The Track

Suggested Time
45–60 minutes

Lesson 12 Overview
Lesson 12 consists of an activity to analyze a popular song by a group with multiple members. After, the students will begin working on the structure of their piece.

Activities

Activity 1
Breaking Down A Track
Analysis of a popular collaborative song

- Students will examine different songwriting terms and how they appear in the selected song

- Students will explore how the structure of a song informs its meaning

Activity 2
Building Up A Track

Group collaboration

Groups will create the structure of their pieces

Materials

- **Students**

  ▸ Beat Rhymers notebooks and writing utensils

- **Instructor**

  ▸ Large writing surface with writing utensils
  ▸ Printed copies of the "Songwriting Terms" handout provided at the end of the lesson.

- Before class, research and print out the lyrics to a popular collaborative song, featuring at least two artists. Make enough copies so that every student can have one. Do your best to pick a song that the students already know. If this isn't feasible, refer to the suggestions below, which we have chosen due to their classic status, and prepare to discuss the collaborative aspects of the track.

- Suggestions:

  ▸ "Uptown Funk" by Mark Ronson, featuring Bruno Mars

    • Mark Ronson produced and co-wrote the track. Bruno Mars sings and performs the track

    • "Empire State of Mind" by Jay Z, featuring Alicia Keys

    • Jay Z raps the verses. Alicia Keys sings the hook and chorus.

  ▸ "Walk this Way" by Aerosmith, featuring Run DMC

    • Aerosmith wrote the track and sings the chorus. Run DMC raps the verses

Activity 1

Breaking Down a Track

Analyzing a popular collaborative track

⏱ Time
15–20 minutes

Setting

Have the groups formed in Lesson 11 get together.

Description

Students will examine different songwriting terms and will reflect on how they appear in the song that you chose. The purpose of this activity is to get students thinking about how the structure of a song informs its meaning.

Exercise

- Discuss the breakdown of different sections in the song: Verses, Intros, Outros, Bridges, Choruses, and Pre-Choruses.

  ▶ How do the different parts of the song connect?

  ▶ Does the song have a message? How and where in the song is it conveyed?

  ▶ What emotions do you feel when you hear the song? Why?

  ▶ When (in what context) would you listen to this song?

- Now initiate a discussion on the collaborative aspects of the song:

  ▶ How many members do you think are in the group?

  ▶ How do they split up the different parts of the song? For example, does each member have their own verse?

  ▶ What does each member of the group bring to the song?

Activity 2

Building Up A Track

A precursor discussion for Unit 3.

⏱ Time
30–40 minutes

Setting

Have the groups formed in Lesson 11 get together and be ready to write.

Description

Students will begin the process of songwriting, specifically working on their song's structure. The class should use the terms from the previous activity and apply them to their own work.

Exercise

- Students will share the free writes they did for homework within their group.

- Once they've shared, they should come up with a song structure. They also should discuss each student's specific role in the song. At this point, you should be walking around the class, sitting in on groups, asking if they need any help.

- Example song structure:

  ▶ 4 bar intro, 16 bar verse, 8 bar hook. 16 bar verse, 4 bar outro.

- Once the groups have decided on their song structure and everyone is clear on what their role is for the song, groups can begin to work on their songs for the rest of the class.

HOMEWORK 🔲

At this point in the class, we recommend that you motivate your students to work on their pieces outside of the classroom, whether within their groups or alone. You do not have to make this work mandatory (in fact it is better if your students are so motivated that they do the work on their own). You should suggest this to your students and offer them ways they can split up the work so they can work alone on their collaborative pieces outside of the class.[14]

---

[14] Unit 3, Lesson 12 Common Core Alignment:
CCSS.ELA-LITERACY.CCRA.L.6–Acquire and use accurately a range of general academic and domain-specific words and phrases sufficient for reading, writing, speaking, and listening at the college and career readiness level; demonstrate independence in gathering vocabulary knowledge when encountering an unknown term important to comprehension or expression
CCSS.ELA-LITERACY.CCRA.SL.1–Prepare for and participate effectively in a range of conversations and collaborations with diverse partners, building on others' ideas and expressing their own clearly and persuasively.
CCSS.ELA-LITERACY.CCRA.SL.2–Integrate and evaluate information presented in diverse media and formats, including visually, quantitatively, and orally.
CCSS.ELA-LITERACY.CCRA.SL.3–Evaluate a speaker's point of view, reasoning, and use of evidence and rhetoric.
CCSS.ELA-LITERACY.CCRA.SL.4–Present information, findings, and supporting evidence such that listeners can follow the line of reasoning and the organization, development, and style are appropriate to task, purpose, and audience.
SMP 1 – Make sense of problems and persevere in solving them
SMP 2 – Reason abstractly and quantitatively

HANDOUT
Songwriting Terms

Introduction

A unique musical passage meant to draw the listener into the song. For example, many Hip Hop producers start off a song with a quote meant to set the tone for the following lyrical material.

Pre-Chorus

A short passage meant to lead into the chorus. Especially in a context when the verses and chorus are on different energy levels, this songwriting device can be useful in making a smoother transition between sections.

Chorus

The chorus usually appears at least more than once throughout the course of the song, and often seeks to distill the subject of the verses into one phrase or stanza. The chorus is often the most distinguished part of the song, and serves to help the listener remember the song.

Verse

The verse carries the details, story, and other more in-depth material that the chorus attempts to distill. A typical song has 2 to 5 unique verses.

Bridge

The bridge is defined by its difference from the Chorus and Verses, and is usually used to break up the repetitive pattern of a song by using different harmonic, rhythmic, or melodic elements.

Solo

Section of a song open for an instrumentalist or vocalist to improvise over.

Outro

How will you end the song? This could be as simple as repeating the last line of the last verse, or as complex as using a new idea to hint at something more.

Lesson 13
Reflection and Revision

Suggested Time
45–60 minutes

Lesson 13 Overview
Lesson 13 consists of a brief discussion on individual student's goals, followed by time for dedicated group work.

Activities

Activity 1
Where Are You On Your Path?

Discussion

- Students will confirm that they are on track with their goals for the collaborative piece

Activity 2
Put In Work

Group work

- Groups will finish writing their songs
- Groups will brainstorm performance elements

Materials

- **Students**
  - Beat Rhymers notebooks and writing utensils
- **Instructor**
  - Large writing surface with writing utensils

Activity 1

Where Are You On Your Path?

A discussion on group progress

Time
Time: 20-30 minutes

Setting

Have the groups get together and be ready to write.

Description

Students will reflect on their song's progress so far. Groups or individuals not on track to complete their songwriting goals will have the opportunity to revise these goals.

Exercise

- Initiate a discussion:
  ▸ What is your song looking like now? How much is finished? What remains?
  ▸ Is each member of your group ready to meet their goals by the end of today's class?
  ▸ Who does not feel like they'll be able to accomplish their goal? Tell us why.
    • "For those who don't feel like you'll be able to finish, what can we do to adjust your goal so that you'll be finished and satisfied by the end of today?"
    • Examples of revised goal: Alter 16 bars to 8, have other students help them with writing
- Note: Remember to revise your record for any

  student that changes their goal.

HOMEWORK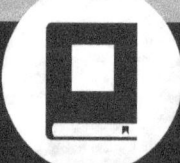

- Short Writing Prompt:
  ▸ What are 3 things I can do to bring our collaboration to life?
    • Answers could include specific dances, ad libs, choices of dress, or other performative elements.
- If any students or groups were unable to meet their goals by the end of the lesson, they must work independently to have them complete by the beginning of next class.[15]

Activity 2

Put In Work

Groups assemble to work on their pieces.

Time
25–30 minutes

Setting

Have the groups get together.

Description

Groups will work towards completing their songs and goals for the collaborative piece. By the end of this lesson, the song should be completely written.

Exercise

- Each group works to finish their song. Take this time to walk around the class checking in and providing help when needed.
- If students finish early, allow time for each group to share their collaborative piece and receive feedback from the rest of the class.

[15] Unit 3, Lesson 13 Common Core Alignment:
CCSS.ELA-LITERACY.CCRA.W.10—Write routinely over extended time frames (time for research, reflection, and revision) and shorter time frames (a single sitting or a day or two) for a range of tasks, purposes, and audiences.
CCSS.ELA-LITERACY.CCRA.L.3—Apply knowledge of language to understand how language functions in different contexts, to make effective choices for meaning or style, and to comprehend more fully when reading or listening.
SMP 6 – Attend to precision
SMP 7 – Look for and make use of structure
SMP 8 – Look for and express regularity in repeated reasoning

Proper Preparation Prevents Poor Performance

Suggested Time
45–60 minutes

Lesson 14 Overview
Lesson 14 consists of a preliminary performance of their collaborative pieces so far, followed by time for revisions.

Activities

Activity 1
Show Don't Tell

Preliminary performance

Students will identify what needs to happen for a song beyond writing

- Students will gain ideas to improve their pieces

Activity 2
Put In Work

Revise and Finalize

- Groups will revise and finalize their writing
- Groups will memorize their pieces
- Groups will develop and practice specific performance tactics to augment their songs
- Groups will rehearse their performances

Materials

- **Students**
  - ▶ Beat Rhymers notebooks and writing utensils
- **Instructor**
  - ▶ Large writing surface with writing utensils

Activity 1

Show Don't Tell

A preliminary performance of the collaborative pieces.

Time
Time: 20-30 minutes

Setting

Have the groups formed in Lesson 11 get together ready to perform.

Tone

This should be an upbeat, fun activity. Keep it lively by encouraging the students to be themselves and be friendly with one another.

Description

Students will be split into their collaborative groups, which will last the entire unit.

Exercise

Students will perform what they have of their pieces. The purpose of this activity is to show what needs to happen for a song beyond writing. The rest of the class will give constructive feedback for each performance. Each group should walk away from this activity with a better idea of what they can add to their performance. While not central to the activity, critiques of writing are permitted as well.

- In this activity, each group will come up to the front of the class and show what they have for their song. For most groups, this could just be reading the verses or choruses they've developed. Others may demonstrate some performance techniques from the homework assignment.

- Again, they may rap or recite their verses.

- After each group performs , engage the class with questions about the fundamentals from Unit 2.

  - How many bars was that group's intro? (If no one knows, have the group go again and count along with them)

  - What literary devices did they use?

  - What was their body language like on stage?

  - What could this group have done improvisationally to improve their performance?

  - Note: Be sure to go over the meaning and importance of constructive criticism with

your class, urging students to articulate the reasons why some aspects of a performance might not be successful. Example of constructive criticism: "The first and second verses sound good, but the second one is off topic."

- After each group performs for the class, give your personal critiques of each and summarize the points that came up most often for the class.

- Discussion:

  - Which groups worked better together and why?

  - Point to performance skills that could enhance their pieces.

  - Groups should all be taking notes on the things they can change about their performance.

Activity 2

Revise and Finalize

A period for students to revise their collaborative pieces

Time
Rest of period

Setting

Have the groups formed in Lesson 11 get together, ready to revise their performances.

Description

Students should have their songs finished by the end of the period. Ideally, most of the work happening during this activity will be performance practice, as all the writing should be finished by now.

Exercise

- Groups spend the rest of the class period working on revisions to their writing and performance.

- If possible, sort out spaces outside the classroom where each group can rehearse privately.

- Suggested Tasks:

  ▶ Finalize all writing.

  ▶ Work on memorization.

▶ Do a "walk-through" of the performance.
Each member of the group just recites the
beginning and last few lines in their verse.
This is to help with transitioning between the
different sections of the songs.[16]

---

[16] Unit 3, Lesson 14 Common Core Alignment:

CCSS.ELA-LITERACY.CCRA.W.3–Write narratives to develop real or imagined experiences or events using effective technique, well-chosen details and well-structured event sequences.

CCSS.ELA-LITERACY.CCRA.W.4–Produce clear and coherent writing in which the development, organization, and style are appropriate to task, purpose, and audience.

CCSS.ELA-LITERACY.CCRA.W.5–Develop and strengthen writing as needed by planning, revising, editing, rewriting, or trying a new approach.

CCSS.ELA-LITERACY.CCRA.L.5–Demonstrate understanding of figurative language, word relationships, and nuances in word meanings.

CCSS.ELA-LITERACY.CCRA.SL.1–Prepare for and participate effectively in a range of conversations and collaborations with diverse partners, building on others' ideas and expressing their own clearly and persuasively.

CCSS.ELA-LITERACY.CCRA.SL.6–Adapt speech to a variety of contexts and communicative tasks, demonstrating command of formal English when indicated or appropriate.

SMP 2 – Reason abstractly and quantitatively

SMP 6 – Attend to precision

SMP 7 – Look for and make use of structure

SMP 8 – Look for and express regularity in repeated reasoning

Lesson 15
Show On the Road

Suggested Time
45–60 minutes

Lesson 15 Overview
Lesson 15 consists of two short performance prep activities followed by the performance of the collaborative piece.

Activities

Activity 1
A Sneak Peak

Group performances

- Groups will perform a snippet of their pieces

- Students will grow more confident in their performances

- The class will determine the show lineup

Activity 2
Showtime!
Groups will perform their pieces in the chosen lineup

Activity 3
Showtime!
Students will discuss their performances

- Students will incorporate feedback

Materials

- **Students**
  - ▶ Beat Rhymers notebooks and writing utensils
- **Instructor**
  - ▶ Large writing surface with writing utensils

Activity 1

A Sneak Peak

A brief snippet of each performance

Time
15–20 minutes

Setting

Have the groups get together, ready to perform.

Description

This activity is an icebreaker to help your students if they are feeling nervous about performing. It's like a performance simulator, in which students go through the motions of a performance without the actual stress of performing the full piece. It also helps students determine the appropriate line-up for the performance.

Exercise

- Each group comes up in front of the class, introduces themselves, shares a few bars from their song, then introducesa the next group.
- The class brainstorms ideas for a first draft of the show lineup, writing it on a large piece of paper to be hung at the front of the room where everyone can see.

Now, allow the groups to rehearse for 10 minutes.

- If any of the groups will be rapping to an instrumental beat, make sure you or one of your students has the music queued up and ready to play on speakers.

Activity 2

Showtime!

A precursor discussion for Unit 3.

Description

It's time for the groups to perform for one another, showcasing the pieces that they've spent the past unit developing.

Tone

Keep the atmosphere positive and respectful. Make sure students clap and show appreciation after every performance. Remind your students that they are all learning, growing, and creating together; reiterate that the Beat Rhymers class is a supportive and respectful environment, and that it's okay to mess up.

Exercise

- Have your students queue their music and solidify the show line-up.
- Be sure all students are prepared to perform. This is also a good time to decide upon the host/MC of the show who will announce and hype up each performance.
- When everyone is ready, alert the class that the show is about to start, and have the first group ready to step up to the stage. Once they begin, try to let the class run the show as much as possible without stopping. Even if students make mistakes, keep the show going! It's important that all groups finish their piece, and introduce the next act on the lineup

Activity 3

The Reviews Are In

A precursor discussion for Unit 3.

Description

Once the students have run through the performance, this discussion activity affords them an opportunity to give and receive feedback to make the show stronger.

Tone

Once your students have gotten through the show, they are past the hard part. The discussion should be relaxed and casual, allowing for a supportive and respectful conversation.

Exercise

When the performances are finished, initiate a discussion with the following questions:

- Discussion Questions:
  - What could we have done better?
  - What did we do well?
  - What did you learn about the songwriting process?
  - Could you have done a whole song by yourself?
  - What can be added to the performance to make it stronger?
  - What is our goal with this performance?
- Be sure that everyone in the class has a turn

to speak and share their thoughts on the performance.

If you have extra time, you can run the performance or any individual pieces again at the discretion of you and your students.[17]

---

[17] Unit 3, Lesson 15 Common Core Alignment:
CCSS.ELA-LITERACY.CCRA.SL.1–Prepare for and participate effectively in a range of conversations and collaborations with diverse partners, building on others' ideas and expressing their own clearly and persuasively.
SMP 1–Make sense of problems and persevere in solving them
SMP 6–Attend to precision

WHAT WORKS
What lessons/activities did your class respond positively to?

STEPS FOR IMPROVEMENT
What lessons/activities need to be modified to be more effective?

_____

_____   _____

_____   _____

_____   _____

_____   _____

_____   _____

_____   _____

_____   _____

_____   _____

_____   _____

_____   _____

_____   _____

_____   _____

_____   _____

_____   _____

_____   _____

_____   _____

_____   _____

NOTES

Any additional notes you'd like to add for this unit?

UNIT 4
INDIVIDUAL SONGWRITING: KNOW THY SELF

Now that your students have gained some songwriting and performance experience, it's time for them to spread their wings! This unit is all about your students taking the skills they've learned thus far to the next level. Not only will they have the chance to work on their own song compositions, but they will decide what kind of project or style they want to pursue in the class. As a facilitator of creative expression, it is important to encourage experimentation and the use of outside musical and performance skills. Without the structure of a group to create accountability, it can be easy for a student to lose his or her way. Make sure all your instructions and expectations are clear at the beginning of each lesson and activity. Students should set achievable goals for themselves to ensure they are met within the given timelines, and always acknowledge the growth and accomplishments of your young people. This is especially crucial now, as this is the first unit where students will begin work on their own content outside of the classroom. Welcome to Unit 4!

Lesson 16
Who Do You Want to Be?

Suggested Time
45–60 minutes

Lesson 16 Overview
In this unit, students will brainstorm ideas for their solo pieces and begin developing their project outlines.

Activities

Activity 1
Choose Your Path
Discussion and free write exercise

- Students will become more comfortable expressing themselves after the instructor presents a work of his or her own

- Students will select a medium of expression for their solo project

Activity 2
Creating The Backbone
Work on individual pieces

- Students will create outlines

- Students will begin writing lyrics

Materials
- **Students**
  - ▸ Beat Rhymers notebooks and writing utensils
- **Instructor**
  - ▸ Large writing surface with writing utensils

Activity 1

Choose Your Path

A brief discussion on finding the right medium of expression

Time
Time: 20-30 minutes

Setting

Students should be seated facing the large writing surface while you take notes on it.

Description

We recommend that you begin this unit by presenting an individual work of your own. If you are a musician or artist of any kind, share one of your pieces. If you are a poet or author, recite a piece of your poetry or prose. If you are a visual artist, present one of your works. Your performance is not mandatory for the class to proceed, but students are often more comfortable expressing themselves when the teacher does the same. After your presentation, the students will be asked to reflect on how they want to express themselves in this unit.

Exercise

Students will perform what they have of their pieces. The purpose of this activity is to show what needs to happen for a song beyond writing. The rest of the class will give constructive feedback for each performance. Each group should walk away from this activity with a better idea of what they can add to their performance. While not central to the activity, critiques of writing are permitted as well.

- On the large writing surface write down a few of the forms of expression students can choose. Here are a few examples:

  ▸ Rapping

  ▸ Singing

  ▸ Spoken word/ Poetry

  ▸ Playing an instrument (Note: It is not your responsibility as a Beat Rhymers Instructor to provide lessons in any instrument beyond what is in this curriculum. However, if your students are already proficient in an instrument and would like to contribute this to the performance, encourage them to do so and to collaborate with their vocalist and lyricist classmates.)

- Once you have written these ideas, ask your students to take out their notebooks, choose one of these artistic practices, and do a 10 minute free write on their connection to and understanding of this medium.

- You can ask them to use "Who, What, When, Where, and Why" of their choices. Remind them that there's no wrong answer in a free write. Here are some specific example questions youth can answer if they get stuck during the freewrite:

  ▸ Who do you respect as an artist working in your chosen form of expression?

  ▸ Why do you like this artist?

  ▸ What does this artist do well? Where do they have room to grow?

  ▸ When would you listen to this artist?

  ▸ Where are certain places or settings where their musical genre would be appropriate? Example: A spoken word artist would be more likely to perform in a coffee shop than a rapper would.

- After they've finished writing, allow a few students to share what path they have chosen and why.

During this time, mention to the class that it's encouraged that they have musical accompaniment for their piece, whether they are rapping, singing, or reciting spoken word. You can provide an instrumental that anyone in the class can use or the students can provide their own.

Activity 2

Creating The Backbone

A preliminary outline for each student's piece

Time
20–30 minutes

Setting

Students should be seated.

Description

Students will begin constructing an outline of their projects

Exercise

- Ask the students to begin brainstorming a song in their notebooks. If they are having difficulty, remind them to use techniques like Word Banks and Bubble Diagrams to get started.

- The students could start out asking themselves what

kind of song (funny, introspective, braggadocio, party) they'd like to make or think about something in their lives that they'd like to speak about.

- Before writing lyrics, have the students construct an outline. Even if they are doing spoken word, they should be able to divide their writing into bars or plan it out into sections so that they have a structure to work within.

If students finish and are satisfied with their outlines, they should begin working on writing their pieces.[18]

---

[18] Unit 4, Lesson 16 Common Core Alignment:

CCSS.ELA-LITERACY.CCRA.W.3—Write narratives to develop real or imagined experiences or events using effective technique, well-chosen details and well-structured event sequences.

CCSS.ELA-LITERACY.CCRA.W.4—Produce clear and coherent writing in which the development, organization, and style are appropriate to task, purpose, and audience.

CCSS.ELA-LITERACY.CCRA.W.5—Develop and strengthen writing as needed by planning, revising, editing, rewriting, or trying a new approach.

CCSS.ELA-LITERACY.CCRA.W.10—Write routinely over extended time frames (time for research, reflection, and revision) and shorter time frames (a single sitting or a day or two) for a range of tasks, purposes, and audiences.

CCSS.ELA-LITERACY.CCRA.SL.6—Adapt speech to a variety of contexts and communicative tasks, demonstrating command of formal English when indicated or appropriate.

SMP 1—Make sense of problems and persevere in solving them.

Laying the Groundwork

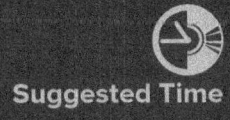

Suggested Time
45–60 minutes

Lesson 17 Overview
Lesson 17 consists of a brief freestyle activity followed by a period for students to work on their pieces.

Activities

Activity 1
Notes Freestyle
Freestyle activity

- Students will generate ideas about their chosen topics for their performances

- Students will explore the motivations, language choices, and emotions related to their performances

Activity 2
Looking Ahead
Work on individual pieces

- Students will set personal goals for the next two lessons

- Students will continue writing their pieces

- Groups will brainstorm performance elements

Materials
- **Students**
  ▸ Beat Rhymers notebooks and writing utensils
- **Instructor**
  ▸ Large writing surface with writing utensils

Activity 1

Notes Freestyle

A freestyle activity to get students started on writing

Time
Time: 15-20 minutes

Setting

Everyone standing in a circle facing inwards so that you are visible to one another.

Tone

This should be an upbeat, fun activity. Keep it lively by encouraging the students to be themselves and be friendly with one another.

Description

Students will form a circle and each student will use their notes and outlines to inspire 8 bar freestyles.

Exercise

- Students are given a minute or so to look over their notes and outlines.

- Once this minute is up, call the class to get into a circle. This activity is going to take the form of "2 Bars and Pass" but more extended. As the class claps, each student will get 8 bars to freestyle on their topics, using their notes as reference. Explain to the students that they can look at their notes, but that in the spirit of true freestyle, they cannot use any of their pre-written lyrics or poetry.

- Again, they may rap or recite their verses.

- After everyone has performed 2 or 3 times, initiate a discussion:

  ▶ Did your freestyle get you thinking about your topic in a different way?

  ▶ What did you learn about freestyling?

  ▶ What changed in terms of your motivation, language choices, or emotions while you were freestyling?

  ▶ Whose freestyle was your favorite? Why?

Activity 2

Looking Ahead

Students will set goals and work on their pieces.

Time
30–40 minutes

Setting

Students should be seated facing the teacher.

Description

Students will establish goals to complete before their performances and continue working on their material.

Exercise

- Explain to the students that setting personal goals and working towards them can be an effective way of organizing their time.

- Let the students know that for the next two lessons, they will largely be working by themselves on their solo pieces. Students will decide on personal work goals for the following days. Students should write the dates of the next two classes in their notebooks, one date at the top of the page, and the other in the middle. At the bottom of the page have them write: "Final Goal: Finished Piece." Everyone should share this goal in common.

- Ask your students to fill in the steps they need to take to reach this final goal. For example, in order to finish by the end of Lesson 19, a student could write that they will have their piece written by the end of Lesson 18. Then in the section for Lesson 19, they could write that by the end of that period they will have memorized as much of their piece as possible.

  ▶ Give the class 5 minutes to write out these goals. Have them raise their hands when finished and go around to check to see that students have set attainable goals.

- After each student is finished, and you've approved their goals, have them start writing. If they are using an instrumental or other pre-recorded music, require that they use headphones as to not distract other students. [19]

[19] Unit 4, Lesson 17 Common Core Alignment:
CCSS.ELA-LITERACY.CCRA.SL.1–Prepare for and participate effectively in a range of conversations and collaborations with diverse partners, building on others' ideas and expressing their own clearly and persuasively.
CCSS.ELA-LITERACY.CCRA.SL.2–Integrate and evaluate information presented in diverse media and formats, including visually, quantitatively, and orally.
SMP 8–Look for and express regularity in repeated reasoning

Lessons 18 and 19
Work Smarter, Not Harder

These two lessons are condensed because they provide uninterrupted creative time for your students to work. These sessions could look very different for individual students. More advanced students will be able to work by themselves without the need for you help, while others may need more guidance. For these lessons, we provide a series of suggested activities meant to stimulate creativity and overcome writer's block. We recommend running at least one of these a day to add some structure to these two lessons.

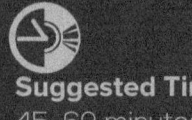

Suggested Time
45–60 minutes

Lesson 18 and 19 Overview
In Lessons 18 and 19, students will work on and finish their individual projects.

Activities

Suggested Activity 1
5 Senses Free Write
5 Senses Free Write

Suggested Activity 2
1-on-1 Practice
Collaborating in groups of 2

Suggested Activity 3
Draw It Out
Drawing activity

Suggested Activity 4
Inspirational Videos
Watching videos

Suggested Activity 5
Journal
Daily journal
Through the suggested activities, students will stimulate their creative process and overcome writer's block

- Students will finish their individual projects

Materials
- **Students**
  - Beat Rhymers notebooks and writing utensils
- **Instructor**
  - Large writing surface with writing utensils
  - Music player (computer, iPhone, anything that can store and play music) and speakers

Suggested Activity 1

5 Senses Free Write

A brief writing activity to stimulate the creative process

 Time
Time: 15–20 minutes

Setting

Students should be seated and ready to write.

Description

Students will participate in a free write describing a personal memory through the 5 senses.

Exercise

- Think of a memory you have that relates to the topic of your song. Think of what you experienced through all five of your senses at that moment in time and take 10 minutes to do a free write on each sense. If you can't remember the exact smells, sounds, tastes, etc., imagine what they might have been.

Suggested Activity 2

1-on-1 Practice

A brief collaborative activity to stimulate the creative process.

 Time
Time: 15–20 minutes

Setting

Pair students off into groups of two. Both students should be at similar levels of completion for their individual pieces.

Description

Have two students work together by performing for each other and giving each other feedback.

Exercise

- The two students should go to a private place where they can freely rehearse and hone their work.

- They should perform for one another, give constructive feedback, discuss their processes, and share writing and performance tips.

Suggested Activity 3

Draw It Out

A brief drawing activity to stimulate the creative process

 Time
15–20 minutes

Setting

Students should be seated at their desks. Choose an instrumental song/album/mix that you think your class will like or let the students vote on one.

Description

Students will use instrumental music as inspiration for drawing. Similar to a free write, this exercise is designed to get students to explore ideas in a loose, unstructured context. Rather than responding to a predetermined written prompt, students are invited to react visually to sound and rhythm.

Exercise

- Inform the students that for the next 15-20 minutes, you will play instrumental music. Similar to a free write, they will be asked to keep working for the full 15-20 minutes. However, instead of writing words, they will draw. It doesn't matter if they're not confident visual artists, the idea is just to get their pens moving. Remind the that the drawing will not be graded and it doesn't matter what it looks like.

- Play the instrumental, and be sure the class stays silent while they draw.

- After the 15–20 minutes have passed, initiate a discussion:

  ▸ How do your drawings relate to your songs?

  ▸ How could your drawings be interpreted as symbols?

  ▸ Could you find some way to relate these symbols to your song?

  ▸ You could also just use your drawings as topics to rhyme about. Are there any places in your song where you were having trouble thinking up rhymes or similes?

Suggested Activity 4

Inspirational Videos

A brief classroom activity to stimulate the creative process

 Time
Time: 15–20 minutes

Setting

Students should be seated facing a monitor or video screen.

Description

Students will be shown inspirational videos about Hip Hop and notable artists to give them ideas and motivate them in the creative process.

Exercise

- Select 10-15 minutes of video clips to show your students.

- These videos can consist of anything related to the artistic process. Remember: they are intended to give the students new ideas and offer new approaches to making music. The videos do not have to be strictly related to Hip Hop. An interview with Freddie Mercury or Stevie Wonder can be just as inspirational.

- Along with the list of movies and videos compiled at the beginning of this guide, we recommend the following:

  ▶ Something from Nothing: The Art of Rap (2012)—Directed by Ice-T and Andy Baybutt. A documentary on the rise of rap music and the artists who made it what it is today.

  ▶ Freestyle: The Art of Rhyme (2000)—Directed by Kevin Fitzgerald, this documentary uses archival footage to show the roots of freestyle rap: from passionate sermons in black churches, to battle rap cyphers on the streets and in formal competitions.

  ▶ Fade to Black (2004)—Directed by Patrick Paulson and Michael John Warren. This documentary, filmed during the "Black Album" era, offers insight into Jay Z's huge success as an MC and entrepreneur in the Hip Hop industry.

  ▶ The Show (1995)—Directed by Brian Robbins. Legends weigh in on the very nature of Hip Hop. Through interviews with some of the biggest names in the game, we get a real glimpse both behind the music and into the industry's inner workings.

  ▶ Rhyme & Reason (1997)—Directed by Peter Spirer. This film forces us to confront the way that listening to Hip Hop music affects our view of ourselves, our community, and each other through extensive interviews with over 80 Hip Hop artists.

  ▶ Planet Bboy (2007)—Directed by Benson Lee. A film about the artform and culture of Bboying, or breakdancing, in urban cultures around the world.

  ▶ Scratch (2002) Directed by Doug Pray. A feature length documentary film about the art form of the DJ and the "turntablist" movement. Of particular note is an interview with DJ Shadow, which can be found on YouTube: https://www.youtube.com/watch?v=1gpKYnRdf0A

  ▶ Rhythm Roulette channel on YouTube— Producers and beatmakers are blindfolded, pushed into a record shop, and asked to select three random records which they must sample to make a track of their own. This is a very unique look into the creative process of Hip Hop producers, and a series that young artists will find particularly engaging.

Suggested Activity 5

Journal

 Time
Ongoing

Setting

Anywhere

Description

Students can keep a daily journal that they can look back on when they are having trouble finding creative material.

If a student is looking for creative inspiration during the class and for the rest of their artistic career, we recommend keeping a daily journal. This journal does not have to have a specific theme or be shown to anyone. It can simply be a collection of brief thoughts, ideas, occurrences, or even drawings. The most meaningful art comes from authentic experience, and keeping a journal offers students a reservoir of sensory experience to tap into for future inspiration.

Exercise

- Challenge the students to record at least 3 thoughts in a journal every day.

- They can simply describe their feelings and basic actions.

- Example: "Today I got into a fight with me mom. It made me feel like she doesn't understand me."

- Remind students that their journals are evolving and are for them to use as ongoing creative resources. In the future, they can look through their journal and find material.[20]

[20] Unit 4, Lessons 18 & 19 Common Core Alignment:
CCSS.ELA-LITERACY.CCRA.SL.5–Make strategic use of digital media and visual displays of data to express information and enhance understanding of presentations.
CCSS.ELA-LITERACY.CCRA.W.3–Write narratives to develop real or imagined experiences or events using effective technique, well-chosen details and well-structured event sequences.
CCSS.ELA-LITERACY.CCRA.W.6–Use technology, including the Internet, to produce and publish writing and to interact and collaborate with others.
CCSS.ELA-LITERACY.CCRA.W.5–Develop and strengthen writing as needed by planning, revising, editing, rewriting, or trying a new approach.
CCSS.ELA-LITERACY.CCRA.W.10–Write routinely over extended time frames (time for research, reflection, and revision) and shorter time frames (a single sitting or a day or two) for a range of tasks, purposes, and audiences.
SMP 8–Look for and express regularity in repeated reasoning

Lesson 20
Express Yourself!

Suggested Time
45–60 minutes

Lesson 20 Overview
Lesson 20 consists of a short performance prep activity followed by student performances and discussion.

Activities

Activity 1
A Closer Look

- Students will practice introducing themselves and share snippets of their performances

- The class will determine a show lineup

Activity 2
Performance Time

- Students will gain confidence in their performance abilities with a full run-through of the show

Activity 3
Community Feedback

- Students will discuss their performances to make the show stronger

Materials

- **Students**
  - ▶ Beat Rhymers notebooks and writing utensils
- **Instructor**
  - ▶ Large writing surface with writing utensils
  - ▶ Music player (computer, iPhone, anything that can store and play music) and speakers

Activity 1

A Closer Look

A brief snippet of each performance

Time
15–20 minutes

Setting
Students should be seated.

Tone
Because many students may be getting nervous at this point, try to make this activity fun and lively. For example, you could have the class clap wildly in support of these flash performances or encourage a joking atmosphere.

Description
This activity is an icebreaker to help your students feel more relaxed. It's effectively a performance simulator, in which students go through the motions of a performance without the actual stress of performing the full piece.

Exercise
- Each student comes up in front of the class, introduces themselves, shares a few bars from their piece, then introduces the next student.

- As a class, quickly come up with the new show lineup and write it on the large writing surface.

Activity 2

Performance Time

For most of the students, this will be their first solo performance. Remember to keep criticism from you and the class constructive. Each student should grow more confident in their abilities through this performance regardless of their skill level.

Tone
Keep the atmosphere positive and respectful. Make sure students clap and show appreciation after every performance.

Even if there are mistakes, keep the show going! It's important that each student finishes their piece and introduces the next act on the lineup. Let the students know that when they are performing, no one in the audience is going to realize if they make a mistake. Have the students brainstorm fun ways to play off mistakes without apologizing or calling attention to them.

Activity 3

Community Feedback

When the performances are finished, initiate a discussion:

- What did we do well?

- What could we have done better?

- Were there ideas or concepts in your song that you found difficult to get across in your performance? Why or why not?

- How do you feel this performance differed from the collaborative one?
  - Were you any more or less comfortable?
  - Did you feel you could express yourself more with this piece and this performance than with the collaborative one?
  - Which did you find easier?
  - Do you feel you would rather be a solo or collaborative artist?

If you have any extra time, you can run the performance again.

Unit 5, Lesson 20 Common Core Alignment:
CCSS.ELA-LITERACY.CCRA.W.10–Write routinely over extended time frames (time for research, reflection, and revision) and shorter time frames (a single sitting or a day or two) for a range of tasks, purposes, and audiences.
CCSS.ELA-LITERACY.CCRA.SL.1–Prepare for and participate effectively in a range of conversations and collaborations with diverse partners, building on others' ideas and expressing their own clearly and persuasively.
CCSS.ELA-LITERACY.CCRA.SL.3–Evaluate a speaker's point of view, reasoning, and use of evidence and rhetoric.
CCSS.ELA-LITERACY.CCRA.SL.4–Present information, findings, and supporting evidence such that listeners can follow the line of reasoning and the organization, development, and style are appropriate to task, purpose, and audience.
CCSS.ELA-LITERACY.CCRA.SL.6–Adapt speech to a variety of contexts and communicative tasks, demonstrating command of formal English when indicated or appropriate.
CCSS.ELA-LITERACY.CCRA.W.8–Gather relevant information from multiple print and digital sources, assess the credibility and accuracy of each source, and integrate the information while avoiding plagiarism.
SMP 1–Make sense of problems and persevere in solving them
SMP 8–Look for and express regularity in repeated reasoning

WHAT WORKS
What lessons/activities did your class respond positively to?

_____

_____

_____

_____

_____

_____

_____

_____

_____

_____

_____

_____

_____

_____

_____

_____

_____

_____

_____

_____

STEPS FOR IMPROVEMENT
What lessons/activities need to be modified to be more effective?

_____

_____

_____

_____

_____

_____

_____

_____

_____

_____

_____

_____

_____

_____

_____

_____

_____

_____

_____

_____

NOTES

**Any additional notes
you'd like to add
for this unit?**

UNIT 5
PERFORMANCE: ROCK THE MIC

Now the participants have tools and experience. They've successfully performed for each other multiple times, they've had the opportunity to hone their writing skills, and they've gotten to know one another. Unit 5 is a chance for the students to focus on the presentation of their artistic selves by further cultivating their performance skills and confidence. While the past units culminated with in-class performances, we recommend that you end the course with one on a bigger scale: perhaps in a school auditorium, community center, or public space. Ending the course this way supports the ultimate goals of giving students artistic autonomy. Students benefit greatly by not only engaging with each other and themselves, but with the greater community. For them to see how their art can affect an audience is essential, no matter if they're singers, MCs, or poets. This being said, there may be students who, having gone through class, decide that performing at a big show isn't for them. This is okay. You should make every effort to include them in activities and performances, but if they are not interested in their own performance, there is no reason to push them to the point of discomfort. There is much in the world of music outside of performance. BEAT students have been hype-men/women, stage managers, costume designers, ghost writers, event promoters, production assistants, producers, audio engineers and more! There are plenty of available roles to fill even if a student decides to forego performance. Several of our participants build up the desire to perform publicly over several semesters after witnessing their peers do so. If a student does not play a role as a lead artist, make sure they are assigned daily tasks that assist instructors or other participants. Encourage all youth to shine in their own special way!

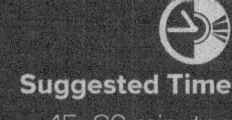

Suggested Time
45–60 minutes

Lesson 21 Overview
Lesson 21 consists of a free write on performance, an activity in which students begin planning their show, and Part One of a two-part activity on proper microphone use.

Activities

Activity 1
How will you rock the crowd?

Free write activity

- Students will reflect on what makes a good performance

Activity 2
Setting The Stage

Collaborative activity

- Students will begin planning their final show
- Students will determine show lineup
- Students will become familiar with the different roles involved in putting on a show
- Students will decide how they want to participate

Activity 3
Microphone Mechanics: part 1

Video and discussion

- Students will learn how to hold the mic
- Students will learn how to control the volume of their vocals through use of the mic

Materials

- **Students**
  - ▶ Beat Rhymers notebooks and writing utensils
- **Instructor**
  - ▶ Large writing surface with writing utensils
  - ▶ Music player (computer, iPhone, anything that can store and play music) and speakers
  - ▶ Projector and adaptor to project videos from computer (if your class is small and they are willing, you can watch the videos from a computer screen, but projector is preferable)
  - ▶ Before class, write a list of the collaborative and solo pieces performed in Units 3 and 4.

Activity 1

How Will You Rock The Crowd?

A free write activity on what goes into a good performance

Time
10–15 minutes

Setting
Students should be seated facing the large writing surface ready to write

Description
Students will do a brief free write about what ingredients add up to a good performance.

Exercise

- Have students do a 7-10 minute free write based on the prompt:

- *"A good performance…"*

- Afterwards, have a few students share their free writes and write them on the large writing surface.

- Examples
  - Has high energy
  - Demonstrates a strong grasp of the material
  - Shows dramatic use of body language
  - Offers effective vocal projection
  - Is entertaining
  - Creates a memory for the audience

Activity 2

Setting The Stage

A brief classroom activity to get the students focused on their upcoming show

Time
25–30 minutes

Setting
Students should be seated facing the large writing surface while you take notes on it.

Description
Students will finalize the show lineup and other details of the show.

Exercise

- Take out the list of the students' performances.

- Explain that they will use the previous exercises to begin planning their final show.

- "Today, we'll be deciding on a show lineup as a class. This will involve each of you making a decision about how you want to be involved. You can create a new solo or collaborative piece, or refine one from earlier in the class."

- If any student feels strongly about not performing, enlist their help for the production of the show. They could be in control of the music, lighting (if applicable), getting people to come out (promotions), or coordinating with the venue staff.

- Once you've outlined these options, give students 5 minutes to quietly look back through their notebooks, reading their lyrics, and recalling their performances. Once they've decided whether they will perform or be a part of production, they should raise their hands and let you know. Write their choices on the large writing surface.

- Use the list of performances to collaboratively decide upon a show lineup. Let the students know they will have opportunities to revise this later.

Activity 3

Microphone Mechanics Part 1

Part one of a two part activity on microphone usage

Time
10–15 minutes

Setting
Students should be seated facing the projector or video screen.

Description
Students will begin to learn how to properly use a microphone.

Exercise

- A very important part of being a vocal artist is to know how to hold a mic.

- Show a few videos of performances (there should be at least one Hip Hop video) that feature an artist using a mic. Recommended:

  ▶ 8 Mile: Eminem's performance in the final battle

- ▶ Tips for a Live Rap Performance : How to Hold a Microphone when Rapping on YouTube, posted by ExpertVillage

- ▶ Any other live performance featuring a professional rapper

- ● After showing the videos, initiate a discussion:

- ▶ What are the performers doing?

- ▶ How are they holding the mic?

- ▶ How do they control the volume of their vocals through use of the mic?

- ● Note: Part 2 of Microphone Mechanics will take place in Lesson 22.

HOMEWORK

Students should begin creating or refining their final song. [22]

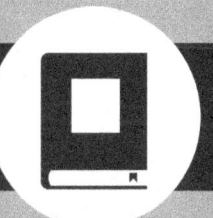

[22]Unit 5, Lesson 21 Common Core Alignment:
CCSS.ELA-LITERACY.CCRA.SL.2—Integrate and evaluate information presented in diverse media and formats, including visually, quantitatively, and orally.
CCSS.ELA-LITERACY.CCRA.SL.6—Adapt speech to a variety of contexts and communicative tasks, demonstrating command of formal English when indicated or appropriate.
CCSS.ELA-LITERACY.CCRA.W.10—Write routinely over extended time frames (time for research, reflection, and revision) and shorter time frames (a single sitting or a day or two) for a range of tasks, purposes, and audiences.
SMP 6 — Attend to precision

Lesson 22
Perfecting Technique

Suggested Time
45–60 minutes

Lesson 22 Overview
Lesson 22 consists of Part 2 of a two-part activity on proper microphone use, followed by an activity in which students will begin to work on transitions between acts for the show.

Activities

Activity 1
Microphone Mechanics: Part 1

Microphone demonstration and practice

- Students will learn more about how to hold and perform with a microphone

Activity 2
Skits and Transitions

Discussion and group work

- Students will work on skits and transitions to changeover between performances during the show

Materials

- **Students**
  ▶ Beat Rhymers notebooks and writing utensils
- **Instructor**
  ▶ Large writing surface with writing utensils
  ▶ Music player (computer, iPhone, anything that can store and play music) and speakers
  ▶ A microphone and amplifier or PA system. As you will need several of these for the final show, secure them at this point so you aren't scrambling to get them before the show starts.
    • This is a matter of access. If you intend to have mics in your final performance, it is very important that students get a chance to practice with them before the actual performance. If you do have access, you should have one for each student in the largest performance group

Activity 1

Microphone Mathematics Part 2

Part two of a two part activity on microphone usage

Time
20–25 minutes

Setting
Students should be seated facing you, and the mic and amp should be set up next to you.

Discussion
Students will learn more about how to use a microphone.

Exercise

Before class begins, set up the microphone and amplifier. It doesn't need to be turned up loud, just enough so that the amplified voice can be heard through the amp/speakers.

To begin, ask students, "who remembers some of the microphone techniques that we discussed during the last class?" Have students demonstrate a few of the concepts and practices they discussed in Lesson 21.

- After this, go over these basics:
  - ▶ One hand should be comfortably gripping the mic while the other holds the cord out of your way to avoid tripping on it.
  - ▶ Microphone Dynamics: The louder you are, the farther the mic should be from your mouth. If you yell directly into it at a close distance, your voice will distort and no one will be able to tell what you're saying. Note how professional singers move their heads back when they hit the high notes.
  - ▶ Because the mic cord will limit your movement around stage, you have to be inventive in using the small amount of space you're given. Think about using levels. Instead of walking to different ends of the stage, you could walk to the right and kneel down towards the crowd, or walk to the left and stand up tall.

- With the mic that you now have set up, ask if any students would like to come up and rap/sing/perform a few bars and demonstrate some of these concepts. If not, do a demonstration yourself. Alternatively, you could do "two bars and pass" with the mic, just working on microphone dynamics.

Activity 2

Skits and Transitions

A period for students to work on skits and transitions between acts.

Time
25–35 minutes

Setting
Students should begin seated facing you, ready to have a discussion.

DiscussionStudents will develop skits to transition between performances during the show.

Exercise

Begin by initiating a discussion:

"There are many different ways that a performer can transition on and off stage. Who can name some?"

Examples:

- ▶ By walking with particular style or swagger.
- ▶ Having a song start before the rapper/singer/poet enters the stage to build anticipation.
- ▶ The artist may address the audience directly and talk about the origin, meaning, or inspiration of the song they are about to perform.
- ▶ The Hype Man/Woman can hop on stage to introduce and acknowledge them.

- After this initial discussion, inform the class that they'll be developing their own skits and creative transitions to be a part of the final show.

- Split the class into groups. Students who will be collaborating on a song performance should be in the same group. While individual performers should develop their own transitions on and off stage, they may also work in concert with larger groups.

- Each group should have their own space or corner of the room.

- These transitions and skits should be quite simple. Give the class 5-10 minutes to come up with their ideas.

For the last few minutes of class students should continue to rehearse their skits. Have the performers share snippets of their performance, focusing on the transitions in between pieces. Whenever a group or individual finishes, they enter the audience and watch the rest of the show. Rehearse as many times as the class-period will permit. In between run-throughs, solicit feedback from students about the efficacy of certain transitions, and allow groups to make small changes when needed.

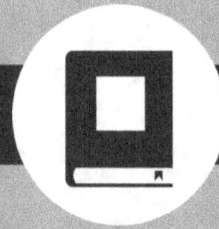

HOMEWORK

Continue working on your final piece. [23]

[23]Unit 5, Lesson 22 Common Core Alignment:
CCSS.ELA-LITERACY.CCRA.W.10—Write routinely over extended time frames (time for research, reflection, and revision) and shorter time frames (a single sitting or a day or two) for a range of tasks, purposes, and audiences.
CCSS.ELA-LITERACY.CCRA.SL.6—Adapt speech to a variety of contexts and communicative tasks, demonstrating command of formal English when indicated or appropriate.
CCSS.ELA-LITERACY.CCRA.SL.1—Prepare for and participate effectively in a range of conversations and collaborations with diverse partners, building on others' ideas and expressing their own clearly and persuasively.
SMP 5 — Use appropriate tools strategically

Lesson 23
Staying Focused

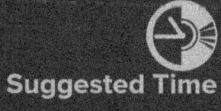

Lesson 23 Overview
Lesson 23 consists of an activity to determine the lineup, followed by a brief period to work on performances.

Activities

Activity 1
Lineup

Discussion

- Students will revise and finalize the lineup for the show

Activity 2
Grinding

Group work

- Students will continue to work on their performances

Materials

- **Students**
  - ▶ Beat Rhymers notebooks and writing utensils
- **Instructor**
  - ▶ Large writing surface with writing utensils

Activity 1

Lineup

A period for students to work on the lineup of the show.

Time
15–20 minutes

Setting
Students should be seated facing the large writing surface while you take notes on it.

Description
Students will the order of performances with transitions.

Exercise

- Address the class: "Today is the last day we're going to be able to work on your pieces in class, so it's important to make full use of our time. To begin, the class will be deciding on the official lineup for the show."

- Write every act on the large writing surface for the students' reference. The students will use this to put together a lineup for the show.

  ▸ Students deserve to have as much control over their show as possible, but as the facilitator, remind them that the flow of acts should be smooth. If there is a student acting as hype-man for one performance, but also

doing their own song, it would make sense to put these two performances next to one another.

- Once the order is set, fill in the transitions that groups and individuals came up with yesterday. Again, make sure everyone is happy with these. Once everyone agrees on them, they're final!

- Keep the lineup information somewhere visible where the students can see it for the rest of the unit.

Activity 2

Grinding

A period for students to work on their upcoming performances.

Time
25–40 minutes

Setting
Students should be in an area where they can work on performing their pieces for the show.

Description
Students will work on their performances.

Exercise

- Address the class: "Next class, we'll be running through everyone's songs to get feedback, so it's important that groups or individuals who are writing a new song be finished with writing by then. Between now and next class, the burden of rehearsal and writing is on you."

- For the rest of class, the students should focus on what needs work. If students need to finish writing, they should do that first.

- Emphasize that while the transitions are important, the actual songs themselves are most important of all, so the students should only move on to practicing their entrances and exits when they feel they're good with everything else.

- While they are working, walk from group to group to see where each one is in their process. If there are still students working on writing, give them more attention and help them figure out the concrete steps they need to take by the end of this class and at home.

HOMEWORK

- For homework, students can work on:

  ▸ Writing their pieces

  ▸ Memorizing the pieces (both hype men/women and performers)

  ▸ Deciding on certain performance techniques to use

  ▸ Transitions

  ▸ Practicing performing for family and friends

  ▸ Finalizing their musical accompaniment [24]

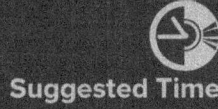

Suggested Time

45–60 minutes

Lesson 25 Overview

Lesson 24 consists of a rehearsal for the final show.

Activities

Activity 1

Rehearsal (On & On)

Performance Rehearsal

- Students will gain confidence in their performance abilities

- Students will have the opportunity to discuss what needs work in their piece and to give constructive feedback to others after each run-through

Materials

- **Students**
  - ▶ Beat Rhymers notebooks and writing utensils
- **Instructor**
  - ▶ Large writing surface with writing utensils
  - ▶ Music player (computer, iPhone, anything that can store and play music) and speakers
  - ▶ Microphones and amplification

---

[24]Unit 5, Lesson 23 Common Core Alignment:

CCSS.ELA-LITERACY.CCRA.W.10—Write routinely over extended time frames (time for research, reflection, and revision) and shorter time frames (a single sitting or a day or two) for a range of tasks, purposes, and audiences.

SMP 1 – Make sense of problems and persevere in solving them

SMP 2 – Reason abstractly and quantitatively

SMP 4 – Model with mathematics

SMP 6 – Attend to precision

SMP 7 – Look for and make use of structure

SMP 8 – Look for and express regularity in repeated reasoning

Activity 1

Rehearsal (On & On)

Time
The whole class period

Setting
Students should be seated in the audience (if you're in an auditorium) or in a group facing the front of the class.

Description
Students will rehearse the entire show.

Try your best to secure a performance space for class today. It doesn't have to be the same one where final show will be, but should be some place that makes this rehearsal seem more official. A stage would be ideal, but if you don't have access, any space will work where you can separate audience and performer.

"Today the class will be running through the show as many times as possible! Everyone should be bringing lots of focus, because not only will you be performing multiple times, but we want to leave time for class feedback at the end of each run-through."

While much of Hop Hop is about performance, it's important that students have a firm grasp of their material. This will also help students to feel confident when taking the stage. For students who haven't learned everything by heart, these dress-rehearsals should serve as an adequate reminder that they need to have their lines memorized. If you feel that there are students in danger of not completing memorization by the next class (which will also be a dress-rehearsal), have a talk with them about shortening their song to make remembering all of their lines easier.

Exercise

● Run through the set. Each student should know the person going on before and after them.

● After you run through it once, make sure you take at least 5-10 minutes for students to share the impressions and feedback for one another.

● Repeat this process as many times as possible until the class period is over. [25]

[25]Unit 5, Lesson 24 Common Core Alignment:
CCSS.ELA-LITERACY.CCRA.SL.1–Prepare for and participate effectively in a range of conversations and collaborations with diverse partners, building on others' ideas and expressing their own clearly and persuasively.
CCSS.ELA-LITERACY.CCRA.SL.2–Integrate and evaluate information presented in diverse media and formats, including visually, quantitatively, and orally.
CCSS.ELA-LITERACY.CCRA.SL.3–Evaluate a speaker's point of view, reasoning, and use of evidence and rhetoric.
CCSS.ELA-LITERACY.CCRA.SL.6–Adapt speech to a variety of contexts and communicative tasks, demonstrating command of formal English when indicated or appropriate.
SMP 4 – Model with mathematics
SMP 6 – Attend to precision
SMP 7 – Look for and make use of structure
SMP 8 – Look for and express regularity in repeated reasoning

Lesson 25
Grow And Prove
Final Rehearsal

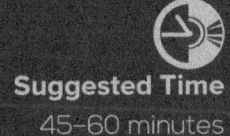

Suggested Time
45–60 minutes

Lesson 24 Overview
Lesson 25 is reserved as a rehearsal for the final show.

Activities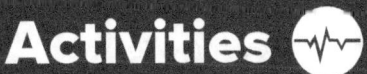

Activity 1
Rehearsal (And You Don't Stop)

Performance Rehearsal

- Students will run through the entire show multiple times to become comfortable with the lineup and their own songs

- The class will get into a performance mindset of confidence and optimism

- Students will understand the logistics of the performance

- At this point do not add any new material only make changes that allow the show to run smoother.

- Reassure participants with positive reinforcement and acknowledgement.

Materials

- **Students**
  ▸ Beat Rhymers notebooks and writing utensils

- **Instructor**
  ▸ Large writing surface with writing utensils
  ▸ Microphones and amplification

Activity 1

Rehearsal (And You Don't Stop)

Students will rehearse their pieces as many times as possible

Time
The whole class period.

Setting
Students should be seated in the audience (if you're in an auditorium) or otherwise in a group facing the front of the class.

Tone
Today is not about revision or critique, it is about getting the class into the right performance mindset. For many of your students, this could be their first time performing. So the most important take-away from today, the last class before the performance, is confidence and optimism. It is more important to point out the parts students did well on rather than erode their confidence by pointing out their mistakes.

Description
Students will spend the entire class period running through the lineup and their individual pieces as many times as possible.

Exercise

- Keeping the above in mind, run through the lineup as many times as possible. Just like a real show, let the students know that even if they make an error, the show must go on. The best thing you can do is to pretend like you didn't make the mistake and the audience will likely never realize.

- No matter what, congratulate and compliment each student after their performance.

- Take the last ten minutes of class to go over any logistical questions that your students might have. Make it clear what they need to bring in, make sure you know what they need for their performances, remind them again of the date, time, and location of the performance.

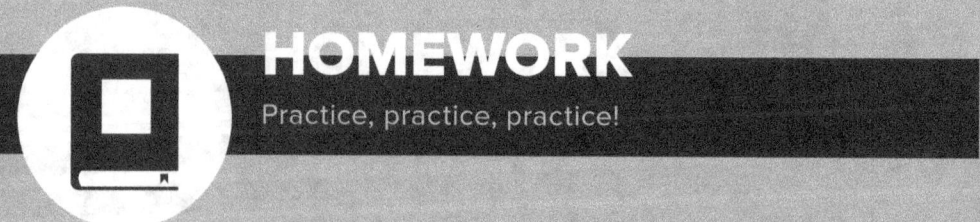

HOMEWORK
Practice, practice, practice!

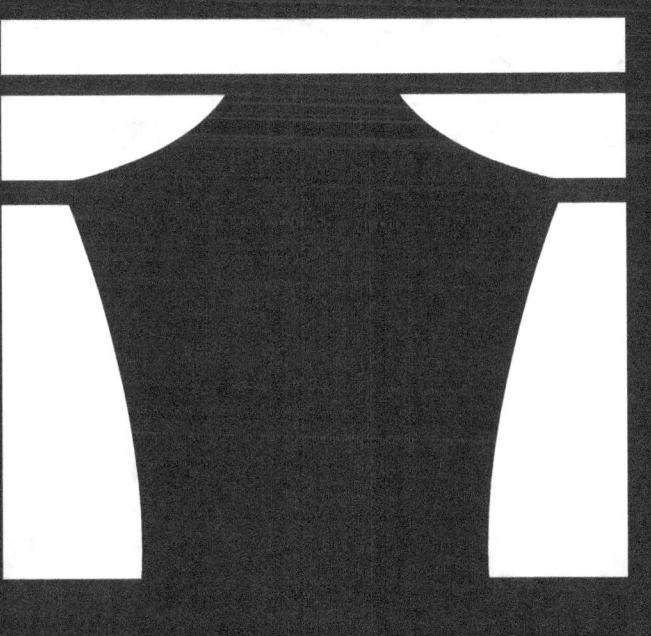

NOTES ON PERFORMANCE

Have your students arrive at least an hour prior to the show so that you can check in on them, make sure that everyone knows their lines, etc.

If there is a student who feels too nervous to perform, remember, it's your job to encourage and support. If they are on the fence, open the space for the other students to encourage and offer positive feedback for the performance. If a student is sure they don't want to perform, there's no reason to force them. Ask them if they'd like to introduce anyone, do half of their song, or participate in the show in a different way.

Before the show starts and the first student on the lineup enters the stage, introduce your class. Keep it brief, but mention to the audience where the class was at the beginning of the year and where they are now. Mention their hard work and the beautiful art they've been able to create. Mention that every verse, every hook, every chorus, and every piece of every song is an original composition created throughout the course of the program. Students should be proud of their accomplishments.

Make sure that you have a student or someone else in charge of queuing any music the students may need.

Finally, sit back and watch. While this may depend on the age of your students, it's important that they have as much ownership over their performance as possible. If you feel that they could get by without you backstage, let them run the show![26]

[26]Unit 5, Lesson 25 Common Core Alignment.
CCSS.ELA-LITERACY.CCRA.SL.1–Prepare for and participate effectively in a range of conversations and collaborations with diverse partners, building on others' ideas and expressing their own clearly and persuasively.
CCSS.ELA-LITERACY.CCRA.SL.4–Present information, findings, and supporting evidence such that listeners can follow the line of reasoning and the organization, development, and style are appropriate to task, purpose, and audience.
SMP 4 – Model with mathematics
SMP 6 – Attend to precision

AFTER THE SHOW

Regardless of how the show went, make sure that all of your students are acknowledged for their hard work and perseverance. They deserve it. To close out this course, we recommend you end with a party or celebration. No activities or structured reflections are necessary (though they certainly shouldn't be forbidden), just a positive atmosphere and some tasty food. Ending the year with such an event helps to provide closure for the students, cementing the course as a positive collective experience in their minds.

Congratulations on the final performance as well as completing this curriculum! We at BEAT would like to thank you for your commitment towards improving the lives of our youth wherever you are. Through implementation of this cypher-based curriculum and through the application of BEAT principles, you have been an instrument of positive change in the lives of your young students. Chances are that this curriculum's unusual methods required you to go outside of your comfort zone as an educator, and for taking this leap of faith, again we thank you. Stay tuned for other curricula and resources at www.beatglobal.org.

Hip Hop Education Resources

Books

- *Pedagogy of the Oppressed by Paulo Freire*
- *Can't Stop Won't Stop: A History of the Hip-Hop Generation by Jeff Chang*
- *The Hip Hop Wars: What We Talk About When We Talk About Hip Hop—and Why It Matters by Tricia Rose*
- *Decoded by Jay-Z*
- *The Gospel of Hip Hop by KRS-One*
- *For White Folks Who Teach in the Hood... and the Rest of Y'all Too: Reality Pedagogy and Urban Education by Chris Emdin*
- *Love, Race, and Liberation; 'Til the White Day is Done edited by JLove Calderon and Marcella Runnell Hall*
- *Conscious Women Rock the Page: Using Hip-Hop Fiction to Incite Social Change by E-Fierce (Creator), Black Artemis (Creator), J-Love Calderon (Creator), and Marcella Runell Hall (Editor)*

Websites

www.daveyd.com

www.rap.genius.com

www.rhymes-with-reason.com

www.hiphopeducation.org

www.literary-devices.com/

www.hiphopadvocacy.org/

Films

- *Wild Style produced by Charlie Ahearn*
- *Rhyme and Reason directed by Peter Spirer*
- *Style Wars directed by Tony Silver*
- *Freestyle: The Art of Rhyme by Kevin Fitzgerald*
- *The Show directed by Brian Robbins*
- *The Hip Hop Project directed by Matt Ruskin*

GLOSSARY

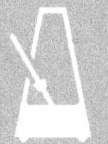

Bar
Commonly referred to a "Measures" in music. A period of time consisting of a specific number of beat.

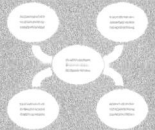

Bubble Diagram
A Bubble Diagram is a visual/drawing with a circle in the middle containing the theme. Smaller circles containing related words branch off the center circle.

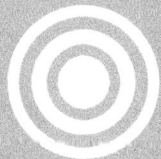

Cypher
A Cypher is gathering of people rapping one after another in the order of the circle they're in. A Cypher can also include dancing, beatboxing, singing, and instruments, but is always held in a circle.

Discussion
Discussions usually follow activities and are a brief follow up on the concepts and skills focused on within the activity. They are a good place to provide as well as receive feedback.

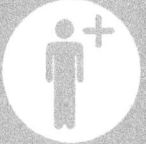

Extension Activity
Extension activities are optional activities designed to supplement the activities provided in each lesson.

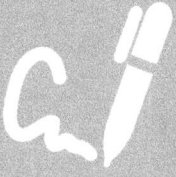

Free Write
Most of the writing activities are Free Writes. Free Writes are stream of conscious writing in which the writer does not edit content, structure, punctuation, or spelling. Free Writes are designed to allow the writer to record a large amount of material without clouding their thinking space by focusing on editing.

Literacy Device
A literary device is a structural tool used by a writer to convey their message to the reader.

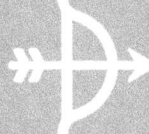

Objective
Each Lesson has at least one objective, a goal you should aim for your class to have accomplished by the end of the lesson.

Word Bank
A Word Bank is a grouping of words that rhyme.

APPENDIX A
ANCHOR STANDARDS FOR READING

Key Ideas and Details
CCSS.ELA-LITERACY.CCRA.R.1

Read closely to determine what the text says explicitly and to make logical inferences from it; cite specific textual evidence when writing or speaking to support conclusions drawn from the text.

CCSS.ELA-LITERACY.CCRA.R.2

Determine central ideas or themes of a text and analyze their development; summarize the key supporting details and ideas.

CCSS.ELA-LITERACY.CCRA.R.3

Analyze how and why individuals, events, or ideas develop and interact over the course of a text.

Craft and Structure
CCSS.ELA-LITERACY.CCRA.R.4

Interpret words and phrases as they are used in a text, including determining technical, connotative, and figurative meanings, and analyze how specific word choices shape meaning or tone.

CCSS.ELA-LITERACY.CCRA.R.5

Analyze the structure of texts, including how specific sentences, paragraphs, and larger portions of the text (e.g., a section, chapter, scene, or stanza) relate to each other and the whole.

CCSS.ELA-LITERACY.CCRA.R.6

Assess how point of view or purpose shapes the content and style of a text.

Integration of Knowledge and Ideas
CCSS.ELA-LITERACY.CCRA.R.7

Integrate and evaluate content presented in diverse media and formats, including visually and quantitatively, as well as in words.

CCSS.ELA-LITERACY.CCRA.R.8

Delineate and evaluate the argument and specific claims in a text, including the validity of the reasoning as well as the relevance and sufficiency of the evidence.

CCSS.ELA-LITERACY.CCRA.R.9

Analyze how two or more texts address similar themes or topics in order to build knowledge or to compare the approaches the authors take.

Range of Reading and Level of Text Complexity
CCSS.ELA-LITERACY.CCRA.R.10

Read and comprehend complex literary and informational texts independently and proficiently.

ANCHOR STANDARDS FOR WRITING

Text Types and Purposes
CCSS.ELA-LITERACY.CCRA.W.1

Write arguments to support claims in an analysis of substantive topics or texts using valid reasoning and relevant and sufficient evidence.

CCSS.ELA-LITERACY.CCRA.W.2

Write informative/explanatory texts to examine and convey complex ideas and information clearly and accurately through the effective selection, organization, and analysis of content.

CCSS.ELA-LITERACY.CCRA.W.3

Write narratives to develop real or imagined experiences or events using effective technique, well-chosen details and well-structured event sequences.

Production and Distribution of Writing
CCSS.ELA-LITERACY.CCRA.W.4

Produce clear and coherent writing in which the development, organization, and style are appropriate to task, purpose, and audience.

CCSS.ELA-LITERACY.CCRA.W.5

Develop and strengthen writing as needed by planning, revising, editing, rewriting, or trying a new approach.

CCSS.ELA-LITERACY.CCRA.W.6

Use technology, including the Internet, to produce and publish writing and to interact and collaborate with others.

Research to Build and Present Knowledge
CCSS.ELA-LITERACY.CCRA.W.7

Conduct short as well as more sustained research projects based on focused questions, demonstrating understanding of the subject under investigation.

CCSS.ELA-LITERACY.CCRA.W.8

Gather relevant information from multiple print and digital sources, assess the credibility and accuracy of each source, and integrate the information while avoiding plagiarism.

CCSS.ELA-LITERACY.CCRA.W.9

Draw evidence from literary or informational texts to support analysis, reflection, and research.

Range of Writing
CCSS.ELA-LITERACY.CCRA.W.10

Write routinely over extended time frames (time for research, reflection, and revision) and shorter time frames (a single sitting or a day or two) for a range of tasks, purposes, and audiences.

ANCHOR STANDARDS FOR SPEAKING AND LISTENING

Comprehension and Collaboration
CCSS.ELA-LITERACY.CCRA.SL.1

Prepare for and participate effectively in a range of conversations and collaborations with diverse partners, building on others' ideas and expressing their own clearly and persuasively.

CCSS.ELA-LITERACY.CCRA.SL.2

Integrate and evaluate information presented in diverse media and formats, including visually, quantitatively, and orally.

CCSS.ELA-LITERACY.CCRA.SL.3

Evaluate a speaker's point of view, reasoning, and use of evidence and rhetoric.

ANCHOR STANDARDS FOR LANGUAGE

Conventions of Standard English
CCSS.ELA-LITERACY.CCRA.L.1

Demonstrate command of the conventions of standard English grammar and usage when writing or speaking.

CCSS.ELA-LITERACY.CCRA.L.2

Demonstrate command of the conventions of standard English capitalization, punctuation, and spelling when writing.

Presentation of Knowledge and Ideas
CCSS.ELA-LITERACY.CCRA.SL.4

Present information, findings, and supporting evidence such that listeners can follow the line of reasoning and the organization, development, and style are appropriate to task, purpose, and audience.

CCSS.ELA-LITERACY.CCRA.SL.5

Make strategic use of digital media and visual displays of data to express information and enhance understanding of presentations.

CCSS.ELA-LITERACY.CCRA.SL.6

Adapt speech to a variety of contexts and communicative tasks, demonstrating command of formal English when indicated or appropriate.

Knowledge of Language
CCSS.ELA-LITERACY.CCRA.L.3

Apply knowledge of language to understand how language functions in different contexts, to make effective choices for meaning or style, and to comprehend more fully when reading or listening.

Vocabulary Acquisition and Use
CCSS.ELA-LITERACY.CCRA.L.4

Determine or clarify the meaning of unknown and multiple-meaning words and phrases by using context clues, analyzing meaningful word parts, and consulting general and specialized reference materials, as appropriate.

CCSS.ELA-LITERACY.CCRA.L.5

Demonstrate understanding of figurative language, word relationships, and nuances in word meanings.

CCSS.ELA-LITERACY.CCRA.L.6

Acquire and use accurately a range of general

academic and domain-specific words and phrases sufficient for reading, writing, speaking, and listening at the college and career readiness level; demonstrate independence in gathering vocabulary knowledge when encountering an unknown term important to comprehension or expression.

ANCHOR STANDARDS FOR MATHEMATICAL PRACTICE

SMP 1: Make sense of problems and persevere in solving them – Mathematically proficient students are able to explain a problem and recognize multiple entry points for finding solution(s). As they work through the problem, they are able to monitor and evaluate their progress and modify their steps if necessary.

SMP 2: Reason abstractly and quantitatively – Mathematically proficient students are able to use their previous knowledge and understanding of mathematical relationships to solve novel problems. They are able to contextualize and decontextualize (represent abstract pieces of math using symbols and/or manipulate parts of the problem as needed) mathematical relationships and understand properties of objects and operations, quantities, and units.

SMP 3: Construct viable arguments and critique the reasoning of others – Mathematically proficient students should be able to talk about math, use mathematical expressions and language, and support or critique others' work. This can be achieved through collaborative tasks, group-based learning experiences, or through presentations.

SMP 4: Model with mathematics – Mathematically proficient students are able to solve real-world problems using the skills and knowledge they have acquired in their math classrooms. Whether counting beats per measure or working with music notes, students will be able to use math to perfect their musical writing and performance skills.

SMP 5: Use appropriate tools strategically—Mathematically proficient students are able to use appropriate tools to make sense of math problems. For example, students need to be able to understand how to operate an amplifier and microphone in order to achieve the fullness of sound required for an effective performance. Students should become comfortable with making these types of decisions over time.

SMP 6: Attend to precision—Mathematically proficient students attend to precision, meaning they are able to solve complex mathematical problems with diligence and exactness. When students are rhyming, freestyling, or counting bars, they need to be able to do so with accuracy and precision in order to achieve the desired effect.

SMP 7: Look for and make use of structure— Mathematically proficient students are able to find patterns and repeated reasoning when they are solving complex problems. Students who recognize these patterns can break problems apart in order to solve them and can integrate new learning into old knowledge.

SMP 8: Look for and express regularity in repeated reasoning—Mathematically proficient students who understand not only minute details, but also the big picture, tend to be able to solve a wide range of problems. These students are able to generalize their thinking and use their reasoning to improve their problem-solving skills, their ability to articulate strategies, and their overall understanding of mathematical concepts.

APPENDIX B
COMMON CORE STATE STANDARDS LESSON ALIGNMENTS

Lesson 1

- **CCSS.ELA-LITERACY.CCRA.W.3**

  Write narratives to develop real or imagined experiences or events using effective technique, well-chosen details and well-structured event sequences.

- **CCSS.ELA-LITERACY.CCRA.W.4**

  Produce clear and coherent writing in which the development, organization, and style are appropriate to task, purpose, and audience.

- **CCSS.ELA-LITERACY.CCRA.W.10**

  Write routinely over extended time frames (time for research, reflection, and revision) and shorter time frames (a single sitting or a day or two) for a range of tasks, purposes, and audiences.

- **CCSS.ELA-LITERACY.CCRA.SL.1**

  Prepare for and participate effectively in a range of conversations and collaborations with diverse partners, building on others' ideas and expressing their own clearly and persuasively.

- **CCSS.ELA-LITERACY.CCRA.SL.6**

  Adapt speech to a variety of contexts and communicative tasks, demonstrating command of formal English when indicated or appropriate.

- **SMP 7**

- **Look for and make use of structure**

Lesson 2

- **CCSS.ELA-LITERACY.CCRA.SL.1**

  Prepare for and participate effectively in a range of conversations and collaborations with diverse partners, building on others' ideas and expressing their own clearly and persuasively.

- **CCSS.ELA-LITERACY.CCRA.SL.2**

  Integrate and evaluate information presented in diverse media and formats, including visually, quantitatively, and orally.

- **CCSS.ELA-LITERACY.CCRA.SL.4**

  Present information, findings, and supporting evidence such that listeners can follow the line of reasoning and the organization, development, and style are appropriate to task, purpose, and audience.

- **CCSS.ELA-LITERACY.CCRA.W.4**

  Produce clear and coherent writing in which the development, organization, and style are appropriate to task, purpose, and audience.

- **CCSS.ELA-LITERACY.CCRA.W.5**

  Develop and strengthen writing as needed by planning, revising, editing, rewriting, or trying a new approach.

- **CCSS.ELA-LITERACY.CCRA.R.1**

  Read closely to determine what the text says explicitly and to make logical inferences from it; cite specific textual evidence when writing or speaking to support conclusions drawn from the text.

- SMP 6

- **Attend to precision**

SMP 7

Look for and make use of structure

SMP 8

- **Look for and express regularity in repeated reasoning**

Lesson 3

- **CCSS.ELA-LITERACY.CCRA.L.1**

Demonstrate command of the conventions of standard English grammar and usage when writing or speaking.

- **CCSS.ELA-LITERACY.CCRA.L.3**

Apply knowledge of language to understand how language functions in different contexts, to make effective choices for meaning or style, and to comprehend more fully when reading or listening.

- **CCSS.ELA-LITERACY.CCRA.L.4**

Determine or clarify the meaning of unknown and multiple-meaning words and phrases by using context clues, analyzing meaningful word parts, and consulting general and specialized reference materials, as appropriate.

- **CCSS.ELA-LITERACY.CCRA.L.5**

Demonstrate understanding of figurative language, word relationships, and nuances in word meanings.

- **CCSS.ELA-LITERACY.CCRA.L.6**

Acquire and use accurately a range of general academic and domain-specific words and phrases sufficient for reading, writing, speaking, and listening at the college and career readiness level; demonstrate independence in gathering vocabulary knowledge when encountering an unknown term important to comprehension or expression.

- **CCSS.ELA-LITERACY.CCRA.SL.2**

Integrate and evaluate information presented in diverse media and formats, including visually, quantitatively, and orally.

- **CCSS.ELA-LITERACY.CCRA.SL.3**

Evaluate a speaker's point of view, reasoning, and use of evidence and rhetoric.

- **CCSS.ELA-LITERACY.CCRA.SL.5**

Make strategic use of digital media and visual displays of data to express information and enhance understanding of presentations.

- SMP 6

- **Attend to precision**

Lesson 4

- **CCSS.ELA-LITERACY.CCRA.L.1**

Demonstrate command of the conventions of standard English grammar and usage when writing or speaking.

- **CCSS.ELA-LITERACY.CCRA.L.2**

Demonstrate command of the conventions of standard English capitalization, punctuation, and spelling when writing.

- **CCSS.ELA-LITERACY.CCRA.SL.1**

Prepare for and participate effectively in a range of conversations and collaborations with diverse partners, building on others' ideas and expressing their own clearly and persuasively.

- **CCSS.ELA-LITERACY.CCRA.SL.6**

  Adapt speech to a variety of contexts and communicative tasks, demonstrating command of formal English when indicated or appropriate.

- **CCSS.ELA-LITERACY.CCRA.W.4**

  Produce clear and coherent writing in which the development, organization, and style are appropriate to task, purpose, and audience.

- **CCSS.ELA-LITERACY.CCRA.W.5**

  Develop and strengthen writing as needed by planning, revising, editing, rewriting, or trying a new approach.

- **CCSS.ELA-LITERACY.CCRA.W.10**

  Write routinely over extended time frames (time for research, reflection, and revision) and shorter time frames (a single sitting or a day or two) for a range of tasks, purposes, and audiences.

- **SMP 6**

- **Attend to precision**

Lesson 5

- **CCSS.ELA-LITERACY.CCRA.W.3**

  Write narratives to develop real or imagined experiences or events using effective technique, well-chosen details and well-structured event sequences.

- **CCSS.ELA-LITERACY.CCRA.W.10**

  Write routinely over extended time frames (time for research, reflection, and revision) and shorter time frames (a single sitting or a day or two) for a range of tasks, purposes, and audiences.

- **CCSS.ELA-LITERACY.CCRA.SL.1**

  Prepare for and participate effectively in a range of conversations and collaborations with diverse partners, building on others' ideas and expressing their own clearly and persuasively.

- **CCSS.ELA-LITERACY.CCRA.SL.6**

  Adapt speech to a variety of contexts and communicative tasks, demonstrating command of formal English when indicated or appropriate.

- **SMP 6**

- **Attend to precision**

Lesson 6

- **CCSS.ELA-LITERACY.CCRA.L.6**

  Acquire and use accurately a range of general academic and domain-specific words and phrases sufficient for reading, writing, speaking, and listening at the college and career readiness level; demonstrate independence in gathering vocabulary knowledge when encountering an unknown term important to comprehension or expression.

- **CCSS.ELA-LITERACY.CCRA.W.10**

  Write routinely over extended time frames (time for research, reflection, and revision) and shorter time frames (a single sitting or a day or two) for a range of tasks, purposes, and audiences.

- **CCSS.ELA-LITERACY.CCRA.SL.2**

  Integrate and evaluate information presented in diverse media and formats, including visually, quantitatively, and orally.

- **SMP 2**

- **Reason abstractly and quantitatively**

  SMP 4

  Model with mathematics

SMP 5

Use appropriate tools strategically.

Lesson 7

- **CCSS.ELA-LITERACY.CCRA.R.4**

Interpret words and phrases as they are used in a text, including determining technical, connotative, and figurative meanings, and analyze how specific word choices shape meaning or tone.

- **CCSS.ELA-LITERACY.CCRA.W.10**

Write routinely over extended time frames (time for research, reflection, and revision) and shorter time frames (a single sitting or a day or two) for a range of tasks, purposes, and audiences.

- **CCSS.ELA-LITERACY.CCRA.L.3**

Apply knowledge of language to understand how language functions in different contexts, to make effective choices for meaning or style, and to comprehend more fully when reading or listening.

- **CCSS.ELA-LITERACY.CCRA.L.5**

Demonstrate understanding of figurative language, word relationships, and nuances in word meanings.

- **CCSS.ELA-LITERACY.CCRA.W.3**

Write narratives to develop real or imagined experiences or events using effective technique, well-chosen details and well-structured event sequences.

- **SMP 6**

Attend to precision

SMP 7

Look for and make use of structure

SMP 8

Look for and express regularity in repeated reasoning.

Lesson 8

- **CCSS.ELA-LITERACY.CCRA.SL.1**

Prepare for and participate effectively in a range of conversations and collaborations with diverse partners, building on others' ideas and expressing their own clearly and persuasively.

- **CCSS.ELA-LITERACY.CCRA.SL.6**

Adapt speech to a variety of contexts and communicative tasks, demonstrating command of formal English when indicated or appropriate.

- **SMP 6**

Attend to precision

Lesson 9

- **CCSS.ELA-LITERACY.CCRA.SL.1**

Prepare for and participate effectively in a range of conversations and collaborations with diverse partners, building on others' ideas and expressing their own clearly and persuasively.

- **CCSS.ELA-LITERACY.CCRA.SL.2**

Integrate and evaluate information presented in diverse media and formats, including visually, quantitatively, and orally.

- **SMP 1**

Make sense of problems and persevere in solving them

- **SMP 6**

Attend to precision

Lesson 10

- **CCSS.ELA-LITERACY.CCRA.SL.1**

Prepare for and participate effectively in a range of conversations and collaborations with diverse partners, building on others' ideas and expressing their own clearly and persuasively.

- **CCSS.ELA-LITERACY.CCRA.L.6**

Acquire and use accurately a range of general academic and domain-specific words and phrases sufficient for reading, writing, speaking, and listening at the college and career readiness level; demonstrate independence in gathering vocabulary knowledge when encountering an unknown term important to comprehension or expression.

- **SMP 1**

Make sense of problems and persevere in solving them

- **SMP 3**

Construct viable arguments and critique the reasoning of others

Lesson 11

- **CCSS.ELA-LITERACY.CCRA.W.5**

Develop and strengthen writing as needed by planning, revising, editing, rewriting, or trying a new approach.

- **CCSS.ELA-LITERACY.CCRA.SL.1**

Prepare for and participate effectively in a range of conversations and collaborations with diverse partners, building on others' ideas and expressing their own clearly and persuasively.

- **CCSS.ELA-LITERACY.CCRA.L.6**

Acquire and use accurately a range of general academic and domain-specific words and phrases sufficient for reading, writing, speaking, and listening at the college and career readiness level; demonstrate independence in gathering vocabulary knowledge when encountering an unknown term important to comprehension or expression.

- **SMP 3**

Construct viable arguments and critique the reasoning of others

- **SMP 8**

Look for and express regularity in repeated reasoning

Lesson 12

- **CCSS.ELA-LITERACY.CCRA.L.6**

Acquire and use accurately a range of general academic and domain-specific words and phrases sufficient for reading, writing, speaking, and listening at the college and career readiness level; demonstrate independence in gathering vocabulary knowledge when encountering an unknown term important to comprehension or expression.

- **CCSS.ELA-LITERACY.CCRA.SL.1**

Prepare for and participate effectively in a range of conversations and collaborations with diverse partners, building on others' ideas and expressing their own clearly and persuasively.

- **CCSS.ELA-LITERACY.CCRA.SL.2**

Integrate and evaluate information presented in diverse media and formats, including visually, quantitatively, and orally.

- **CCSS.ELA-LITERACY.CCRA.SL.3**

Evaluate a speaker's point of view, reasoning, and use

of evidence and rhetoric.

- **CCSS.ELA-LITERACY.CCRA.SL.4**

  Present information, findings, and supporting evidence such that listeners can follow the line of reasoning and the organization, development, and style are appropriate to task, purpose, and audience.

- **SMP 1**

  Make sense of problems and persevere in solving them

- **SMP 2**

  Reason abstractly and quantitatively

Lesson 13

- **CCSS.ELA-LITERACY.CCRA.W.10**

  Write routinely over extended time frames (time for research, reflection, and revision) and shorter time frames (a single sitting or a day or two) for a range of tasks, purposes, and audiences.

- **CCSS.ELA-LITERACY.CCRA.L.3**

  Apply knowledge of language to understand how language functions in different contexts, to make effective choices for meaning or style, and to comprehend more fully when reading or listening.

- **SMP 6**

  Attend to precision

  SMP 7

  Look for and make use of structure

- **SMP 8**

  Look for and express regularity in repeated reasoning

Lesson 14

- **CCSS.ELA-LITERACY.CCRA.W.3**

  Write narratives to develop real or imagined experiences or events using effective technique, well-chosen details and well-structured event sequences.

- **CCSS.ELA-LITERACY.CCRA.W.4**

  Produce clear and coherent writing in which the development, organization, and style are appropriate to task, purpose, and audience.

- **CCSS.ELA-LITERACY.CCRA.W.5**

  Develop and strengthen writing as needed by planning, revising, editing, rewriting, or trying a new approach.

CCSS.ELA-LITERACY.CCRA.L.5

  Demonstrate understanding of figurative language, word relationships, and nuances in word meanings.

- **CCSS.ELA-LITERACY.CCRA.SL.1**

  Prepare for and participate effectively in a range of conversations and collaborations with diverse partners, building on others' ideas and expressing their own clearly and persuasively.

- **CCSS.ELA-LITERACY.CCRA.SL.6**

  Adapt speech to a variety of contexts and communicative tasks, demonstrating command of formal English when indicated or appropriate.

- **SMP 2**

  Reason abstractly and quantitatively

- **SMP 6**

Attend to precision

- **SMP 7**

Look for and make use of structure

SMP 8

Look for and express regularity in repeated reasoning

Lesson 15

- **CCSS.ELA-LITERACY.CCRA.SL.1**

Prepare for and participate effectively in a range of conversations and collaborations with diverse partners, building on others' ideas and expressing their own clearly and persuasively.

- **SMP 1**

Make sense of problems and persevere in solving them.

- **SMP 6**

Attend to precision.

Lesson 16

- **CCSS.ELA-LITERACY.CCRA.W.3**

Write narratives to develop real or imagined experiences or events using effective technique, well-chosen details and well-structured event sequences.

- **CCSS.ELA-LITERACY.CCRA.W.4**

Produce clear and coherent writing in which the development, organization, and style are appropriate to task, purpose, and audience.

- **CSS.ELA-LITERACY.CCRA.W.5**

Develop and strengthen writing as needed by planning, revising, editing, rewriting, or trying a new approach.

- **CCSS.ELA-LITERACY.CCRA.W.10**

Write routinely over extended time frames (time for research, reflection, and revision) and shorter time frames (a single sitting or a day or two) for a range of tasks, purposes, and audiences.

- **CCSS.ELA-LITERACY.CCRA.SL.6**

Adapt speech to a variety of contexts and communicative tasks, demonstrating command of formal English when indicated or appropriate.

Lesson 17

- **CCSS.ELA-LITERACY.CCRA.SL.1**

Prepare for and participate effectively in a range of conversations and collaborations with diverse partners, building on others' ideas and expressing their own clearly and persuasively.

- **CCSS.ELA-LITERACY.CCRA.SL.2**

Integrate and evaluate information presented in diverse media and formats, including visually, quantitatively, and orally.

- **SMP 8**

Look for and express regularity in repeated reasoning.

Lesson 18 and 19

- **CCSS.ELA-LITERACY.CCRA.SL.5**

Make strategic use of digital media and visual displays of data to express information and enhance understanding of presentations.

- **CCSS.ELA-LITERACY.CCRA.W.3**

Write narratives to develop real or imagined experiences

or events using effective technique, well-chosen details and well-structured event sequences.

- **CCSS.ELA-LITERACY.CCRA.W.6**

Use technology, including the Internet, to produce and publish writing and to interact and collaborate with others.

- **CCSS.ELA-LITERACY.CCRA.W.5**

Develop and strengthen writing as needed by planning, revising, editing, rewriting, or trying a new approach.

- **CCSS.ELA-LITERACY.CCRA.W.10**

Write routinely over extended time frames (time for research, reflection, and revision) and shorter time frames (a single sitting or a day or two) for a range of tasks, purposes, and audiences.

- **SMP 8**

Look for and express regularity in repeated reasoning

Lesson 20

- **CCSS.ELA-LITERACY.CCRA.W.10**

Write routinely over extended time frames (time for research, reflection, and revision) and shorter time frames (a single sitting or a day or two) for a range of tasks, purposes, and audiences.

- **CCSS.ELA-LITERACY.CCRA.SL.1**

Prepare for and participate effectively in a range of conversations and collaborations with diverse partners, building on others' ideas and expressing their own clearly and persuasively.

- **CCSS.ELA-LITERACY.CCRA.SL.3**

Evaluate a speaker's point of view, reasoning, and use of evidence and rhetoric.

- **CCSS.ELA-LITERACY.CCRA.SL.4**

Present information, findings, and supporting evidence such that listeners can follow the line of reasoning and the organization, development, and style are appropriate to task, purpose, and audience.

- **CCSS.ELA-LITERACY.CCRA.SL.6**

Adapt speech to a variety of contexts and communicative tasks, demonstrating command of formal English when indicated or appropriate.

- **CCSS.ELA-LITERACY.CCRA.W.8**

Gather relevant information from multiple print and digital sources, assess the credibility and accuracy of each source, and integrate the information while avoiding plagiarism.

- **SMP 1**

Make sense of problems and persevere in solving them

- **SMP 8**

Look for and express regularity in repeated reasoning

Lesson 21

- **CCSS.ELA-LITERACY.CCRA.SL.2**

Integrate and evaluate information presented in diverse media and formats, including visually, quantitatively, and orally.

- **CCSS.ELA-LITERACY.CCRA.SL.6**

Adapt speech to a variety of contexts and communicative tasks, demonstrating command of formal English when indicated or appropriate.

- **CCSS.ELA-LITERACY.CCRA.W.10**

Write routinely over extended time frames (time for research, reflection, and revision) and shorter time frames (a single sitting or a day or two) for a range of tasks, purposes, and audiences.

- SMP 6

  Attend to precision.

Lesson 21

- **CCSS.ELA-LITERACY.CCRA.W.10**

  Write routinely over extended time frames (time for research, reflection, and revision) and shorter time frames (a single sitting or a day or two) for a range of tasks, purposes, and audiences.

- **CCSS.ELA-LITERACY.CCRA.SL.6**

  Adapt speech to a variety of contexts and communicative tasks, demonstrating command of formal English when indicated or appropriate.

- **CCSS.ELA-LITERACY.CCRA.SL.1**

  Prepare for and participate effectively in a range of conversations and collaborations with diverse partners, building on others' ideas and expressing their own clearly and persuasively.

- **SMP 5**

  Use appropriate tools strategically.

- **SMP 6**

  Attend to precision

Lesson 22

- **CCSS.ELA-LITERACY.CCRA.W.10**

  Write routinely over extended time frames (time for research, reflection, and revision) and shorter time frames (a single sitting or a day or two) for a range of tasks, purposes, and audiences.

- **SMP 1**

  Make sense of problems and persevere in solving

them

- **SMP 2**

  Reason abstractly and quantitatively

  SMP 4

  Model with mathematics

- **SMP 6**

- **Attend to precision**

  SMP 7

- **Look for and make use of structure**

  SMP 8

  Look for and express regularity in repeated reasoning

Lesson 23

- **CCSS.ELA-LITERACY.CCRA.W.10**

  Write routinely over extended time frames (time for research, reflection, and revision) and shorter time frames (a single sitting or a day or two) for a range of tasks, purposes, and audiences.

- **SMP 1**

  Make sense of problems and persevere in solving them

- **SMP 2**

  Reason abstractly and quantitatively

  SMP 4

  Model with mathematics

- **SMP 6**

- **Attend to precision**

SMP 7

- **Look for and make use of structure**

SMP 8

Look for and express regularity in repeated reasoning

Lesson 24

- **CCSS.ELA-LITERACY.CCRA.SL.1**

Prepare for and participate effectively in a range of conversations and collaborations with diverse partners, building on others' ideas and expressing their own clearly and persuasively.

- **CCSS.ELA-LITERACY.CCRA.SL.2**

Integrate and evaluate information presented in diverse media and formats, including visually, quantitatively, and orally.

- **CCSS.ELA LITERACY.CCRA.SL.3**

Evaluate a speaker's point of view, reasoning, and use of evidence and rhetoric.

- **CCSS.ELA-LITERACY.CCRA.SL.6**

Adapt speech to a variety of contexts and communicative tasks, demonstrating command of formal English when indicated or appropriate.

- **SMP 4**

Model with mathematics

- **SMP 6**

Attend to precision

SMP 7

Look for and make use of structure

SMP 8

Look for and express regularity in repeated reasoning

Lesson 25

- **CCSS.ELA-LITERACY.CCRA.SL.1**

Prepare for and participate effectively in a range of conversations and collaborations with diverse partners, building on others' ideas and expressing their own clearly and persuasively.

- **CCSS.ELA-LITERACY.CCRA.SL.4**

Present information, findings, and supporting evidence such that listeners can follow the line of reasoning and the organization, development, and style are appropriate to task, purpose, and audience.

- **SMP 4**

Model with mathematics

- **SMP 6**

Attend to precision

APPENDIX C
ENGLISH LANGUAGE ARTS ACTIVITY ALIGNMENTS

Strand	Core Skills	Musical Activities/ Lessons
Reading for Literature	• Recount narratives, folk tales, etc. • Understanding words and phrases that describe rhythm & meaning • Determine structure of a story • Understand characters' points-of-view • Identify who is telling story • Compare and contrast two stories, or different versions of a story (e.g., text vs. media) • Determine and analyze theme • Make connections between written text and other perspectives	• Folk songs • Rhythms, patterns, repetition, form • Form • Texture & balance • Timbre (melody/harmony) • Theme & variations • Programmatic composition • Cultural connections to music
Reading for Information	• Analyze details of a text • Meaning of domain specific words • Describe overall structure of events, ideas, or concepts • Distinguish own point-of-view from others' • Engage in group reading with purpose and understanding	• Critical listening • Expressive markings in music • Music-specifivvc vocabulary • React to music, improvisation • Sing and play with others
Reading for Foundational Skills	• Phonics and word recognition • Fluency—write and read with ease comfort	• Read music notation, follow own part • Sound production, diction, articulation • Lyrics, rhythm, note reading/recognition • Music reading, practice for fluency
Writing	• Write and express opinions supporting one's views • Draw evidence from text for analysis • Write information/explanatory texts • Produce and edit own writing Short research projects • Write to support analysis of topics or text • Create text in response to literary work	• Critical responses, written critiques • Reflection, improvement plan • Short research projects • Music critiques • Music composition
Speaking & Listening	• Ask/answer questions to clarify comprehension • Create multimedia presentations of texts/poems • Engage in collaborative discussions • Evaluate speaker's point-of-view • Integrate multimedia to clarify information • Make strategic use of digital media	• Critical listening for performance in ensemble • Create audio recording of performance • Rehearsals, peer evaluation, group composition • Analyze music composition • Use music software/technology in composition • Enhance composition/performance through media
Language	• Connect word meanings and their uses • Correct use for frequently confused words • Use knowledge of language to write, speak, read, and listen • Use nuances in word meanings • Acquire and use domain-specific words •Demonstrate command of standard English	• Musical vocabulary • Clarify misused vocabulary in music • Correctly use music terminology to describe music • Expressive quality of lyrics • Write or speak about music • Phrasing, articulation, expression markings

MATH ACTIVITY ALIGNMENTS

Strand	Core Skills	Musical Activities/ Lessons
Counting & Cardinality	• Know number names and counting sequences	• Know rhythmic value of notes and rests • Count basic rhythms
Operations & Algebraic Thinking	• Represent addition/subtraction with objects • Generate and analyze patterns	• Math problems using note values • Performance of rhythmic/tonal patterns • Musical form
Number & Operations-Fractions	• Understand fractions as numbers • Understand fraction equivalents	• Rhythmic values of notes and rests • Meter • Measures • Rhythm pyramid (whole, half, quarter, etc.)
Measurement & Date	• Counting • Work with time • Measure lengths • Describe and compare measurements • Represent and interpret data	• Time signature • Organize sound over time (rhythmic aspect) • Tempo • Intervals • Science of sound (frequency, amplitude, etc. of sound waves)
Geometry	• Identify and describe shapes • Graph points to solve real-world problems • Making inferences and justifying conclusions from observation	• Form • Melodic contour • Timbral and pitch qualities of sound, voice, acoustics etc.
Speaking & Listening	• Ask/answer questions to clarify comprehension • Create multimedia presentations of texts/ poems • Engage in collaborative discussions • Evaluate speaker's point-of-view • Integrate multimedia to clarify information • Make strategic use of digital media	• Critical listening for performance in ensemble • Create audio recording of performance • Rehearsals, peer evaluation, group composition • Analyze music composition • Use music software/technology in composition • Enhance composition/performance through media
Ratio & Proportional Relationships	• Ratio concepts and use reasoning to solve problems	• Linear arrangement of rhythmic relationships • (create melodies, etc.) • Lining up rhythms between parts

AUTHORS

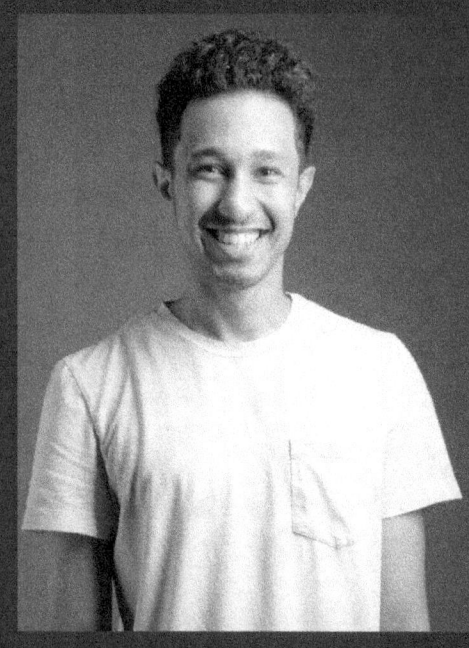

Yogi Guyadin

Yogi Guyadin, or Y?, is a multifaceted artist, audio engineer/producer, and educator born in NYC. His artistic journey began through through creative writing and poetry. As an Emcee, Y? has performed at notable venues such as The Blue Note Jazz Club, Highline Ballroom, and S.O.B's. He studied Audio Engineering and Music production, and has completed internships and assistant engineering positions at "Electric Lady Studios" and "Manhattan Center." Feeling the need to serve his community, Y? began volunteer instructing Music Production/Songwriting classes in the housing projects of Queens. These programs led Yogi to work with nonprofit organization and teachers in the Department of Education. He began building mobile studios and developed various student-based music programs around the concept of "cypher-based pedagogy."Students learn music and writing fundamentals through collaboration, the classroom is turned into a stage where youth express themselves regardless of prior artistic experience. Currently Y? works with BEAT Global as teaching artist and program director. He instructs the Beat Makers course and has created two programs: Beat Rhymers (a creative/songwriting program for aspiring poets, emcees and singers) and Beat Band (a live music course where students compose and produce original music and songs alongside professional musicians). To expand artistically, Y? Studies instruments and vocals in order to create music of various genres. He is the co-owner of The Space station studios in Queens and an active member of Playback NYC (an improv theater company). Y? is a student of life whose mission is to show love and grow through the same creative collaboration he brings to the youth. For more info please visit **www.whynotshowlove.com**

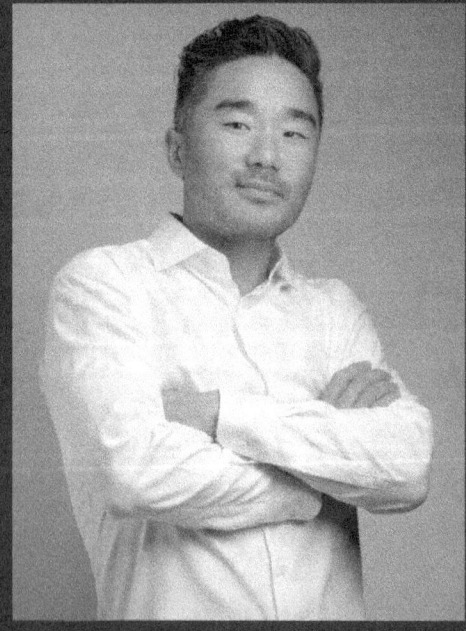

James Kim

James Kim, Executive Director of Bridging Education & Art Together (BEAT), comes from a professional event marketing background, which started at Comedy Central and MTV. James has produced myriad events including premiere parties for The Chappelle Show, HBO Comedy Festival in Aspen and the New York-Tokyo Music Festival. In 2005, he co-founded a brand-marketing agency, Catharsis NYC, where he helped incubate and launch various pioneering events. Currently, James is the co-producer for the R-16 World Bboy Master Championships, one of the largest Hip Hop/bboy events held annually in Seoul, Korea. After touring the UK with legendary Bboy icon, Ken Swift and the VII Gems Rock Division in 2009, James began to recognize a void of Hip Hop in the educational system. He began devising an after-school program that focused on the spirit of Hip Hop, taught by experienced and pioneering figures of the movement. In the Spring of 2010, he launched Beat Breakers, a Bboy/Bgirl program at the Bronx Academy of Letters, with Ken Swift as the Director and Bboy WaAak1 as Head Instructor. Deeply moved and inspired by the students at the LaVelle School for the Blind in the Bronx, James enlisted the help of beatboxing powerhouses Taylor McFerrin, Adam Matta, and Chesney Snow, and launched Beat Rockers in 2009. With the success and positive reception of both Beat Breakers and Beat Rockers, James added an additional program called Beat Makers with producer, DJ and composer, Dhundee, which focuses on music production. In 2012, yet another program focusing on poetry, spoken word, MC'ing and production was born featuring MC, musician, and poet Y?. These four programs serve as the foundation for BEAT James continues to nurture and grow engaging programs in order for youths in the underserved communities of New York City to have a voice, learn new skills, and be inspired by the professionals who teach them.

Human

Human is the Creative Crusader who grows with purpose and strives to be a disruptive innovator and agent of change. His NYC-based "make tank," Human Developments is focused on harnessing the power of the diverse arts and visually cultivating a collective of creatives at the crossroads of photography and graphic design solution for collaborative discovery, innovation and change. His deep experience in brand strategy and creative thinking is accountable for the modern re-imagining of brand and identity platforms that meet the strategic needs and visions of young social entrepreneurs and clients who dream awake. Human also spends much of his time advancing a nationwide dialogue on how to help father figures persist, recover and thrive amid the disruption the present court system offers. Over the past six years, he has been the Founding Photografather of DAD IS A VERB, an unprecedented pro-social advertising initiative utilizing his artistic sensibilities to touch, move, and inspire dads everywhere to be extraordinary. For more info visit **human.carbonmade.com**

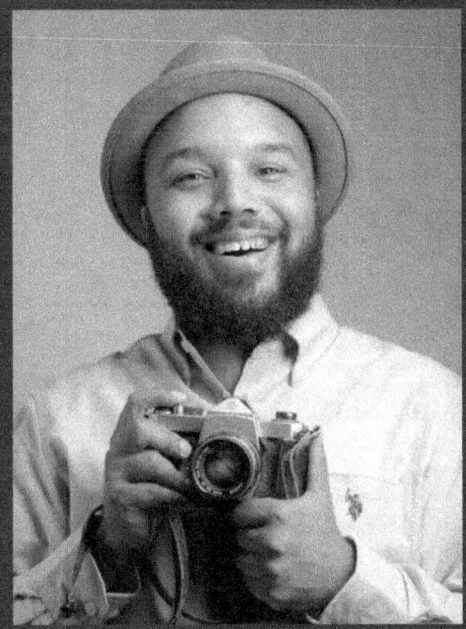

JLove Calderón

JLove is an activist, author, coach and a creator, producer and director of TV and Film. Her short films, ASIA-ONE: Expect The Unexpected, and From Gangs to Gardens, have garnered an audience of over 18 million viewers. She co-produced 11:55 Holyoke, a feature film by Ben Synder and Ari Issler. JLove has co-created, executive produced and directed five TV pilots including M1's The Message featuring Joey Bada$$, The Sound of Revolution, Breaking Bias with Grammy Award winning J.Ivy, We The People with Michael K Williams and received distribution for their Hip-Hop Rising Series on Virgin Airlines "In-Flight Entertainment." She consults with organizations and companies as a Social Impact Strategist connecting and curating innovative, transformative products, live events and experiences with a triple bottom line impact: people, planet, profit. **www.jlovecalderon.com**

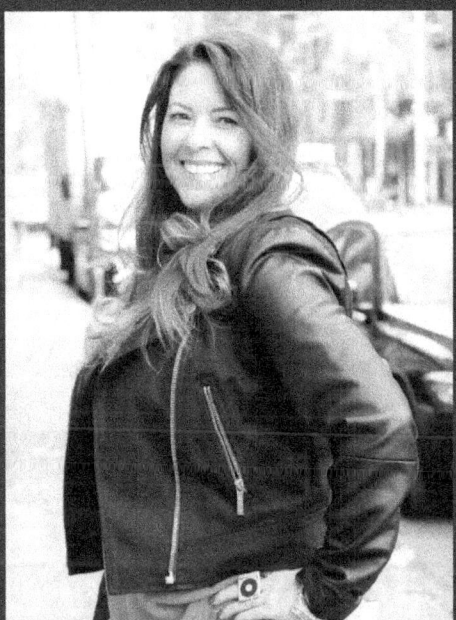

Shirley Torho

Shirley Torho unearthed her passion for community organizing and activism as an undergraduate at Barnard College and a graduate student at Columbia University's Mailman School of Public Health, where she worked on numerous initiatives, including curriculum reform, developing and facilitating a cultural sensitivity training for Higher Education Opportunity Program staff, structuring prevention programs to address disproportionate access to education and health care in underserved communities, and serving as the Program Coordinator at the Intercultural Resource Center, a residential community aimed at exploring diversity issues on and around campus. Over the years, Shirley has presented her work in various spaces, including innovation hubs such as Summit Series, a collection of entrepreneurs and other change-makers committed to social change. She's also participated on panels addressing the integration of arts, health, and education as a tool for holistic healing in traumatized communities with the likes of film and music producer, Quincy Jones III (QD3), and worked with the United Nations Foundation on the My World 2015 Campaign. Currently, Shirley is the Manager of Course Development at Advancement Courses, a company that seeks to improve student achievement by creating asynchronous, graduate-level courses that help teachers enhance their practice and careers, and consults for The Research Masters, where she's developed content for major publishing companies, including McGraw-Hill, Pearson, and Barrons.

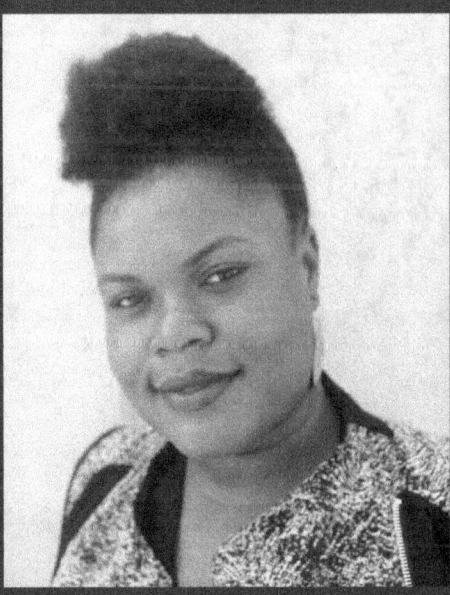

BEAT RHYMERS CURRICULUM EDITING TEAM

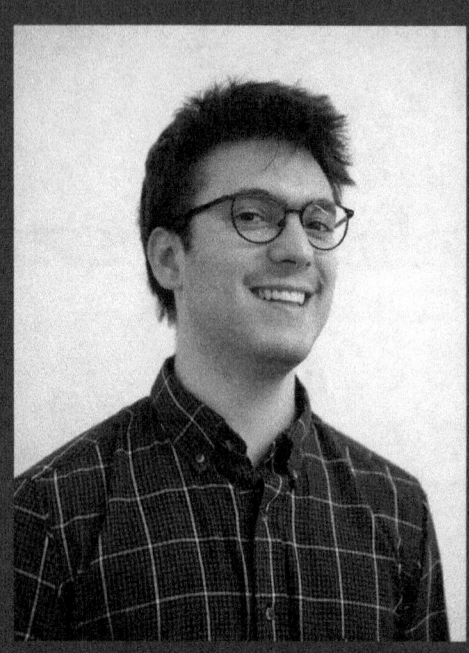

John Tournas

John Tournas is a musician, anthropologist, and aspiring educator. A recent graduate of Harvard College, he produced written and sonic essays based primary research of the Boston Hip Hop scene. He was also the Music Director of CityStep, a student-run volunteer organization that teaches dance and creative expression to children in the Cambridge Public School system. John spends his time making beats, playing the saxophone, and collaborating artistically with as many people as he possibly can. He feels blessed to be working at BEAT., where he can combine his two passions: music and community outreach.

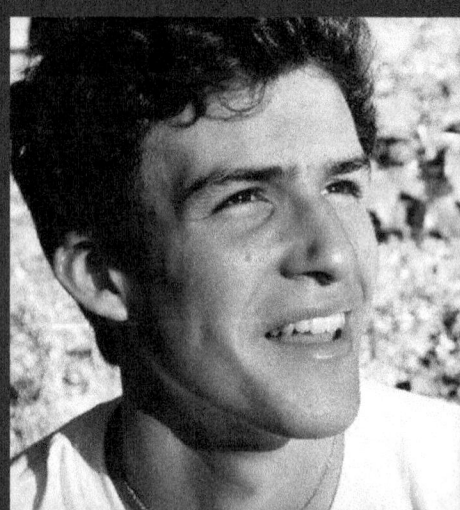

Richard Hauser, Jr.

Richard is a philosophy major at Fordham University and aspiring music producer. He grew up in Queens, where he developed a passion for Hip Hop that he would like to share with the community through nonprofit work and arts education. He is currently taking Ableton Live production classes at Dubspot on behalf of the Matthew Steven Azar Scholarship.

Anna Diorio

Anna Diorio, also known as Happy Accident, is a writer, singer, MC, pianist, and cultivator of community striving everyday to spread positive vibrations for the greatest good of all sentient beings. Anna's artistic and healing practice seeks to uplift and inspire the spirit, bridge the gap between intuition and intellect, and facilitate the transformation of pain into creative expression. Ms. Diorio is deeply rooted in a long lineage of Jazz musicians, and her branches in Hip Hop are a natural extension of a deep love for poetry, global community, and intuitive musicality. Anna is grateful to be a part of the BEAT family, which nourishes creative expression for all ages. For more information, please visit **www.annamdiorio.com**

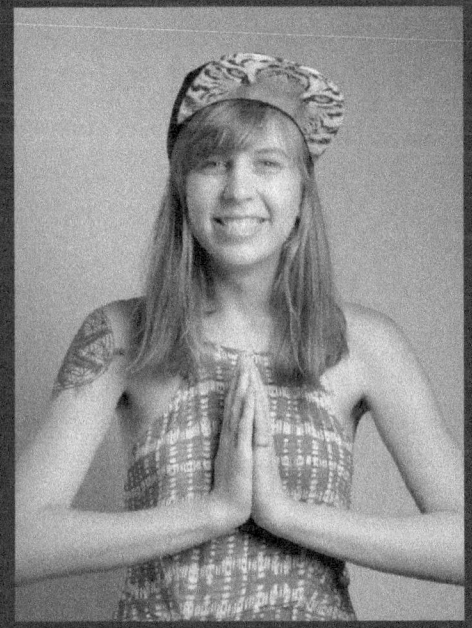

Cecilia Cruz

Cecilia is an educator at heart and is passionate about using her skills to help people achieve success and wellbeing. She has worked in education and training in academic, non-profit, healthcare, government, and international settings and has spent fifteen years studying and working in Europe and Asia. She's also a yoga instructor and yoga therapist with a focus on empowering underserved people such as veterans, older adults, and disadvantaged communities. Cecilia believes we are all called to contribute our individual strengths to help create a world that is more peaceful and just. With a Master's degree in Education and experience in curriculum development, instructional design, and teaching, volunteering with Bridging Education & Art Together (BEAT) as a curriculum editor was a natural fit for her. She strives to make a positive difference wherever she is as this allows her to give back for all the opportunities and gifts she has been given. Cecilia also enjoys hiking, creative writing, and the company of her cats.

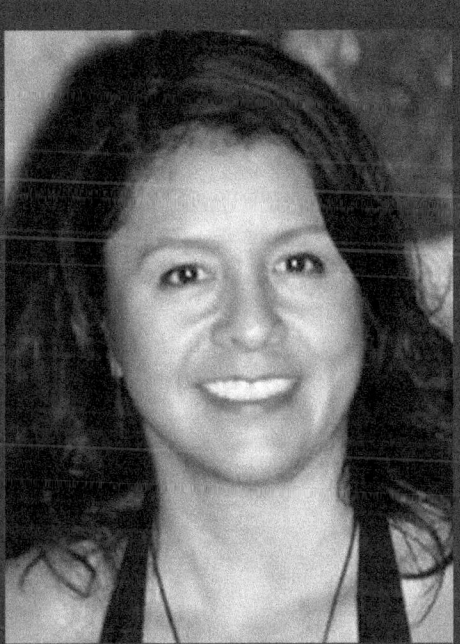

Matia Burnett

Matia Madrona Burnett is a writer, editor, and educator originally from Washington State, where she grew up on a farm. After earning a Master of Education degree in Oregon, she taught writing, reading, and job skills to homeless youth and adult refugee students. In 2007, Matia left the West Coast for New York City to study writing at Columbia University. She now works as a journalist, editor, and children's book reviewer for the Manhattan-based company, Publishers Weekly. Music is always running through Matia's head and some of her favorite memories are of singing around campfires growing up. She also plays piano and (just a little) guitar and feels very strongly about the importance of music and all arts education in schools. Some of her other interests include geology, art and photography, making fruit pies, swimming in oceans and lakes, walking around cities at night, and all kinds of animals.

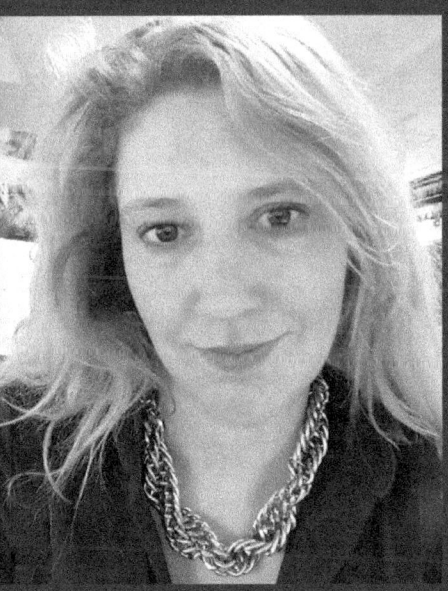

NOTES

NOTES

NOTES

NOTES

NOTES

SEE WHAT STUDENTS ARE SAYING!

"This program is important to me because I feel like it's not everyday that we can express ourselves, whether it's through music or through anything, so [this] is a great outlet for me personally. It's a place when I have a scattered brain, I feel like I can organize my thoughts. I can really make my aspirations and goals reachable [...] Public speaking... that's the number one thing it's helping me with. Also, just socializing. When you learn to collaborate you learn to just talk to people, and that really helps a lot."
— **Daniel,** *Beat Rhymers Graduate, East Side Community High School*

"It actually kind of helped me kind of find a productive way to get over my depression, and it actually helped me get to know my fellow students and I created a lot more friendships through Beat Rhymers."
— **Alice,** *Beat Rhymers Graduate, East Side Community High School*

"I feel like BEAT has helped me to grow—not only musically, but as a person. Putting me on stage, and things like that and making me a co-facilitator of a whole classroom... that sort of thing pushes you to just be more comfortable with yourself. BEAT has helped me develop social skills that I didn't have before, as a young dude. I was very introverted, and now I'm not."
— **LJ,** *Beat Rhymers Graduate, East Side Community High School*

"Students that once cut my class have become the most dedicated performers. I see students transform from scared and shy to empowered and prolific"
—**Y?,** *BEAT Global Arts Coordinator*

BEAT

For more information on our programs, products, and
curricula for today's youth, visit beatglobal.org